THE TARPON BOOK

A Complete Angler's Guide

by

Frank Sargeant

Book III in the Inshore Series

A LARSEN'S OUTDOOR PUBLISHING BOOK
THE ROWMAN & LITTLEFIELD PUBLISHING GROUP. INC.
Lanham ▪ Chicago ▪ New York ▪ Toronto ▪ Plymouth, UK

Published by
LARSEN'S OUTDOOR PUBLISHING
An imprint of The Rowman & Littlefield Publishing Group, Inc.
4501 Forbes Boulevard, Suite 200, Lanham, Maryland 20706
http://www.rlpgtrade.com

Estover Road, Plymouth PL6 7PY, United Kingdom

Distributed by National Book Network

British Library Cataloguing in Publication Information Available

Library of Congress Cataloging-in-Publication Data Available

Library of Congress 91-76442

ISBN: 978-0-936512-16-4 (paper : alk.paper)

♾™ The paper used in this publication meets the minimum requirements of American National Standard for Information Sciences—Permanence of Paper for Printed Library Materials, ANSI/NISO Z39.48-1992.

Printed in the United States of America

ACKNOWLEDGEMENTS

Expert tarpon anglers from throughout silver king country were kind enough to share their lives and their secrets with me in the preparation of this book. Captains Ray DeMarco, Harlan Franklin, Paul Hawkins, Mike Locklear, Bill Miller, Kenny Shannon, Earl Waters and Jon Zorian were particularly instructive and generous. Also very helpful were captains Lee Baker, Dave Ballay, Charlie Cleveland, Al Dopirak, Dave Markett, Larry Mendez, and Scott Moore. Many members of the Boca Grande Guides Association and the Florida Keys Guides Association also contributed significantly, as did Billy Pate, perhaps the world's finest and most persistent flyrod tarpon angler.

In Costa Rica, Archie Fields of Rio Colorado Lodge was a gracious host and instructor. Biologists Roy Crabtree of the Florida Department of Natural Resources and Randy Edwards of Mote Marine Laboratories deserve all the credit for the sections on the biology and migration of tarpon. And Bob Hewes, the guru of flats boats, provided many of the insights for the boating chapter. Finally, thanks to Stu Apte--one of the great pioneers of the sport--who was kind enough to take a young hopeful under his wing and offer a bit of encouragement on the Homosassa flats 20 years gone by.

Cover illustration of a battling tarpon is by St. Petersburg, Fla., artist and guide Russ Sirmons. Sirmons sculpts his exquisite works in glass with sandblasting equipment, translating what he sees on the water into accurate and exciting art that captures both the anatomical details and the spirit of his subjects. He accepts commissions for fish and birds of all species. His telephone number is (813) 526-2090.

3

PREFACE

This is a book about the tarpon, Megalops atlanticus, also known as the silver king, and in Central and South America as the sabalo. Whatever you call the silver giant, there are no words to describe his performance when hooked. Most world-ranging anglers agree, the tarpon is the ultimate light tackle fish, besting even the Atlantic salmon for its aerial displays, its power, and its heart. The beauty of its best-known habitat, the clear, shallow flats of the tropics, also adds to the vote for the tarpon as number one.

The book is a collection of the knowledge of dozens of truly fine tarpon fishermen, many of them acknowledged as among the world's best. It covers finding and catching tarpon in all the vast varieties of range and habitat it enjoys, and details the use of all types of tackle for outwitting this big-eyed, big-scaled, silver giant.

The tarpon's ready availability to the inshore angler makes it unique among the big-game fish, those commonly reaching more than 100 pounds. The giant silver king can be hooked as readily by the bridge and pier fisherman as by the fly-rod expert on the flats or by the sportsman trolling from the stern of a million-dollar yacht. He's a democratic cuss, just as happily shattering drug-store spincasters as $700 fly outfits, and he's as likely to pop up 50 miles up a freshwater river as 100 miles into the Gulf of Mexico.

Tarpon have experienced the same stresses on their habitat as many other inshore species in the last 40 years, but seem to have weathered it well in many areas. They are still remarkably abundant in most of their range, and connecting with that first silver king--a high point in the growth of most anglers--is easy for anyone who takes the time to learn the basics.

The body of knowledge on tarpon is growing by tarpon-sized leaps as this text is written, with exciting new research projects revealing the secrets of biology and migration that had only been guessed at formerly. You'll find much in THE TARPON BOOK that has been printed nowhere else, much that hopefully will make you an admirer, as well as a more successful pursuer, of this unique resident of our coastal seas.

(EDITOR'S NOTE: Limits and other management rules mentioned throughout THE TARPON BOOK were current at printing time, but are subject to change by state and federal fishery councils. Check local laws before fishing in your area.)

CONTENTS

ABOUT THE AUTHOR

Frank Sargeant is outdoors editor of the Tampa Tribune and a senior writer for Southern Outdoors, Southern Saltwater and BassMaster magazines. He was formerly an editor for CBS Publications, and a writer for Disney World Publications, as well as southern editor for Outdoor Life. His writing and photos have appeared in a wide variety of other publications, including Field & Stream, Sports Afield, Popular Mechanics, Popular Science and The Reader's Digest. He was a fishing guide before becoming a writer and editor. He holds a masters degree in English and Creative Writing from Ohio University, and has taught writing at the high school and college level. His works have won more than 40 national awards in the past decade. He is also author of the companion volumes THE SNOOK BOOK and THE REDFISH BOOK. Sargeant lives on the Little Manatee River, near Tampa, Florida.

CHAPTER 1

INTRODUCTION

SEVEN BIG GREEN TORPEDOES, coming at you in a deadly spread. Seven giant fish, carved of stainless steel, bright as swords.

Lucky seven?

Maybe lucky, this time.

The fly line sings through the guides, the fly whistles past your ear on the final ride out to the end of the leader.

For once the cast falls right, the slick fatness of the monocore turning over the 3/0 fly just right to fall with a gentle ripple on the clear surface.

Strip it in, the line sliding between forefinger and the cork grip, short, sharp strips that make the cockroach pattern breath, dance in the slow tide.

The second fish rolls a big eye at it, fixes on it, turns her heavy head toward it as she peels out of the school.

She follows, five feet from the fly, now three, now a foot.

Tease her. Two little twitches.

The tarpon opens the gallon-bucket of a mouth and inhales it. You wait that long second for her to turn sideways, back to join her companions, then tighten the line, feel the ponderous weight, and snatch the point home with a mighty tug on the line and a powerful strike with the big 12-weight rod.

And then the whole world blows up.

The fish goes up in a twisting, head-shaking, gill-rattling explosion of saltwater, towering up there against the noon-day sun, higher than your head, painting herself forever against that tropic sky, and then she falls back with a crash like a locomotive going off the end of a dock, and you are doing a mad ballet on the front deck, trying to dance that hissing fly line out from under your bare feet and get her on the reel. The last coils go up, hitting the rod with a crack, and then the reel starts to sing as the last of the line and then the backing start to go in a long arc, following the fish, now leaping again, and now again, off through the sea. Congratulate yourself. The heart has stood it, yet again. There is absolutely nothing in fishing that matches it, those first few moments when a giant tarpon feels the hook and goes ballistic.

It's an addictive business, one that has lead men to spend fortunes, marriages, lifetimes in the pursuit. Like most addictions, it feeds on itself, and there is no such thing as enough, for the afflicted.

Tarpon are everyman's fish, as likely to pop up in the middle of a turbid, urban harbor in downtown Miami as to flex their silvery backs on the air-clear grass flats of the Florida Keys. Their range spans the Central Atlantic along the shores of three continents, making them the most widely distributed of any inshore gamefish. In part responsible for this distribution is their remarkable ability to breath air, just as you and I. They take it in the characteristic "roll" at the surface, gulping it down into an air bladder that is richly supplied with blood vessels, just as our lungs are. Thus, tarpon can survive in water with little oxygen, in areas that kill other fish quickly.

They are perhaps the world's greatest angling target, combining incredible length and bulk with an astonishing acrobatic ability, great endurance and an indomitable spirit. They are true big-game fish, yet can be caught from the smallest of boats, and even from shore. They are incredibly powerful, yet are susceptible to capture by the most basic tackle in skilled hands. And they are among the most primitive of fish, yet possess remarkable beauty and grace.

But this is not a book given to the mystique and mystery of the tarpon. There are plenty of those already on American bookshelves. Instead, (with a one-chapter exception) this is a nuts-and-bolts book, a book of mechanics, not poetry, designed

Tarpon reach enormous sizes, yet are often found within casting distance of shore, and always within range of nearly any small boat.

to teach the beginner how to begin, to find and catch his first tarpon. Hopefully, it will also burnish the shield of the expert a bit, with points on the fine-tuning of tackle and techniques so that he connects more consistently, wins the battles more frequently.

We live in an era when many of the secrets of the tarpon are just being uncovered, both by more good anglers than have ever before pursued the species, and by the work of marine biologists who are finally getting funding for tarpon research projects, much of it generated by saltwater fishing licenses and in at least one case, by a special tarpon tag required for sportsmen to harvest a fish.

Much of what is known about tarpon, both by anglers and scientists, has come to light within the last decade. This new knowledge, and the growing respect for this unique species, means we can expect good fishing for this ancient fish to continue into the next century.

CHAPTER 2

TARPON COUNTRY

ATLANTIC TARPON ARE FOUND in an amazing variety of inshore tropic and subtropic waters throughout the central Atlantic. There are even a few Pacific tarpon, pioneers through the Panama Canal, though their population is limited to the locks. Tarpon thrive in such a diversity of water types that there is no classifying what constitutes "likely" tarpon water. The snook angler can take one look at a mangrove shore and pronounce it "snooky", but there's no telling where tarpon might pop up, or where they won't.

Tarpon are found from the thousand-foot indigo depths of the continental shelf (during the spawn) to the most polluted blackwater harbors, surviving happily in water that would kill most other species in minutes. They show up in water that's completely fresh, a hundred miles from the nearest sea, as well as in water too salty for many fish to survive.

The juveniles are found in abundance in completely landlocked ponds in coastal areas, with golf course water-hazards a prime rearing area in many parts of Florida. Mosquito canals and roadside ditches are also prime habitat for young tarpon. A few even show up among the largemouth bass in Lake Okeechobee, and they occasionally surprise catfish anglers by gulping bottom baits 20 miles up Florida's Apalachicola River.

Classic water for mature tarpon is clear and shallow, like that throughout the Florida Keys, the nation's best and hardest-fished area. The deeper flats of Homosassa, on

Tarpon are found in a wide variety of habitats, but classic water is the clear shallows of the tropic flats. Here, sight-fishing is possible, and a hooked fish puts on an incredible acrobatic display.

Florida's west-central coast, are also world-renowned for jumbo tarpon. There are fair to good tarpon flats along much of the east coast of Central America, particularly in areas like Belize, where the barrier islands create clear, shallow lagoons inviting to fish and fishermen.

These are the Rolex-class waters, necessary for flyrod success. But far more tarpon are seen and caught in deeper waters, some of it swift and clean like the 70-foot depths of Boca Grande Pass, green water that boils along at speeds up to six knots--and some of it still, black backwaters like those of Charlotte Harbor, or the murky creeks of the Everglades or South and Central America, or the outflows of electrical generating plants from Fort Lauderdale to Naples, or the polluted inner-city ship basins at Tampa and Miami.

They prowl the gentle surf of most of Florida's Gulf coast from May through October--and they show up by the hundreds in the more rugged seas of the Atlantic shores, particularly during the fall mullet run from St. Augustine southward.

Dark, tannin-stained waters also hold tarpon regularly. The fish adapt to an amazing variety of waters due to their ability to breath atmospheric oxygen. The range extends throughout the tropics and sub-tropics on both sides of the Atlantic.

In U.S. waters, tarpon are found in catchable numbers as far north as Cape Hatteras in summer. There are also good numbers of them in the waters of South Carolina and Georgia during the warmer months. All of Florida is tarpon water from May through October, but during winter, they're found in dependable numbers only in the rivers in the southern half of the peninsula, with the best fishing from Fort Lauderdale southward on the east coast, and from Naples down through the Keys on the western shore.

In the Gulf of Mexico, tarpon fishing is primarily a summer sport. Excellent numbers are found in the Grand Isle/Venice area of Louisiana, particularly in August, September and early October. Tarpon are also taken around the shrimp rigs in Texas, often providing excellent action for those who chum with the so-called "by-catch" of unwanted fish and crabs. They rarely show up inshore in Texas these days, though there was a good bay fishery for them there historically.

From the Mexican border southward, tarpon become increasingly abundant, particularly in areas where jungle rivers

17

flow into the Caribbean. There are huge concentrations in Costa Rica, particularly just outside the bar at the Rio Colorado. The tarpon don't run to giant sizes, with the average fish about 60 pounds, big ones 100 pounds, but their abundance is remarkable at times. The fish are also found well up the rivers here at times, though not quite so abundant as they once were. Nicaragua, now enjoying more stable relations with the U.S., reportedly has an untapped fishery in the inshore lagoons.

Belize also has lots of fish and several well-developed camps for recreational anglers. Tarpon are found both in the muddy jungle rivers and in the clear flats around the outside islands. Fair-to-good numbers of tarpon also exist at river outflows throughout the remainder of Central America and on around the bend of South America to central Brazil. The world all-tackle record, a 283-pounder, was caught from Lake Maracaibo in Venezuela in 1956. Islands offshore of South America, including Los Roques, also have plenty of fish.

They're also found landlocked in several large lakes on the Cayman Islands, in the green rivers of Jamaica, and in modest numbers around many other of the Caribbean islands which have steadily flowing rivers.

Really big tarpon, over 200 pounds, are abundant nowhere on Earth--with one evident exception. The coast of Gabon, in East Central Africa, has produced six IGFA line-class record fish of more than 200 pounds since 1980. Fishing facilities are reportedly primitive here and the fish are found in murky, open water making the pursuit a lot less enjoyable than an encounter on clear, shallow flats. But for a really good shot at a giant, Africa is presently the place to go--if you've got a yen for adventure, plenty of money, and plenty of time to try working out fishing arrangements on your own.

In short, so long as you find water temperatures of 75 degrees or warmer, it's harder to name spots where tarpon won't appear than where they will. The one constant for a stable tarpon population is a sizable estuarine area where the young can grow toward maturity. Without this brackish habitat--increasingly rare due to shoreline development in much of the U.S. range--tarpon populations cannot thrive.

CHAPTER 3

NATURAL BAITS

THE SHORTEST LIST in the world is a list of live baits that tarpon will NOT eat.

Blue crabs? They love 'em, the bigger the claws, the better.

Saltwater catfish? No problem, poisonous spines and all.

Gafftops? The "slime monsters" are gulped down with relish.

Eels? Slither and slide and slip right in.

Tarpon eat just about all small creatures that live in the sea. The only qualifier is that the dinner must fit down their throat whole, since they have no teeth to bite their food into chunks.

They eat anything, but some items seem to be on the preferred list. Scaled sardines, threadfin herring and menhaden or "shad" are favorites on the west coast of Florida. On the east coast and in the Florida Keys, mullet are a staple. In the Carolinas and along the Georgia coast, menhaden again get the nod.

At Boca Grande in spring and early summer, the main course is made up of the small brown "pass crabs" that float through the pass on the new and full moon tides.

When the fish go into coastal rivers in summer, blue crabs make up a main portion of their diet.

Also high on the food list are ladyfish--a fairly close relative of the tarpon--and both spotted and silver seatrout. They love croakers and pigfish and pinfish as well.

Shrimp are a favorite of juvenile fish, and even the biggest female won't turn down a drifting jumbo. In fact, it's not unlikely that the success of fly-fishermen is based on this preference, since the popular "cockroach" pattern looks much like a shrimp in color, size and action.

They eat all of the above baits dead as well as alive, and love nothing better than the assorted "by-catch" of mixed fish, crabs, shellfish and bottom junk that comes off the back of a shrimp boat.

Sheepshead anglers occasionally see them working up the chum line of barnacles they scrape off bridges.

They even reportedly eat bananas! Legend is that in days gone by, large numbers gathered around the banana boat docks in Tampa harbor and gulped down every stray banana that fell over the side during offloading.

I caught one in the Homosassa River on a wiener, once. (Hey, it was before I became a purist.)

So what WON'T a tarpon eat?

Maybe stingrays, although I wouldn't put it past them.

Finding And Storing Bait

An oversized livewell with a powerful flow-through seawater system is an essential in fishing live bait for tarpon, because the most attractive baits, including scaled sardines, threadfins and mullet, require lots of clean, aerated water for survival. The well should have rounded corners so the baits keep swimming instead of stacking up in the corners, and a large, removable screen over the outflow, so that seaweed and scales can be cleaned off regularly.

Sardines and threadfins are found along beaches and the edges of grassflats, usually in "green" or clear water. They can be spotted by the "shad ripple" they create on the surface as they feed, tiny splashes that look like a very localized rain shower. (Watch out for schools of "yellow jackets", tiny mackerel-like fish with poisonous stinging spines, that look very similar from the surface. Though tarpon would probably eat them, they're too nasty to clear out of the net and get on a hook to be used as bait.)

A small-mesh monofilament castnet is the ticket for catching these baits. The best size is 8 to 12 feet, expensive to

20

A castnet is a basic tool for the live bait angler, whether he selects mullet, sardines, threadfin or menhaden to offer to the silver king. Choose one with a large diameter and extra weights on the lead line.

buy, big to handle, but far more effective than the smaller, cheaper nets because it traps a much larger area. Nets open to about twice their nominal size, and the more area you cover, the more fish are caught underneath as the school dives and flares. Good nets have lots of big weights along their bottom, too--the faster the net sinks, the more baits you catch.

Sardines come to a chum mix of canned jack mackerel, canned sardines in oil, and whole wheat bread, all softened to a paste with sea water. Bits of the mix are trickled over the stern to lure them into range. Threadfins won't come to the chum, and are generally caught by gliding up to them on motor power and throwing the net from the bow.

Incidentally, thread herring can be caught over deep water with a heavy cast net--they don't have to be trapped against bottom. The trick is to make the throw, let the net freefall the length of the line, and then purse it very sharply to close the bottom on any baits caught in the upper folds.

Sardines are more active on the hook and more durable than threadfins, so are the preferred bait of the two.

Menhaden or "shad" look similar to the thread herring, but get a lot bigger, up to a foot long. They're found in areas of high nutrient concentration--the back sections of Tampa Bay produced millions of pounds for years before commercial purse seiners cleaned out the stocks. They're also found, in great numbers, along the beaches of the Carolinas and Georgia, where the big rivers provide abundant feeding areas.

21

Menhaden can also be caught in a large castnet, again by "motorfishing" them over deep water. They survive reasonably well in a live well if not crowded.

Mullet are prime tarpon bait where ever they are found. The little "finger" sized models, 4 to 5 inches long, are located up tidal creeks all summer in most areas where tarpon live, and are not tough to net if approached via wading, or in a boat manipulated by trolling motor or push pole.

Larger mullet are also great tarpon bait, particularly along the east coast during the late summer and fall mullet migrations southward. There, millions of mullet move just off the beach, making an easy target for a wading castnetter. Individual mullet are often caught with large treble snatchooks, simply by jerking the hook through the schools.

Mullet do well in large live wells, so long as they are kept cool and not crowded. They require lots of oxygen, but not necessarily a constant supply of raw water--they'll survive overnight in an iced, closed system with lots of aeration.

Crabs can be scooped up along the beaches after dark, caught in traps baited with fish remains, or netted in open water as they swim along the surface. In Boca Grande, thousands of them swim at the surface during the spring and summer migrations.

The nice thing about crabs is that they require very little attention once caught. They don't need an aerated well, and do best if kept in a shaded bucket with an inch of water in the bottom and a handful of seaweed or a piece of wood so they can climb up. They can survive for long periods on atmospheric oxygen, so don't need to be submerged, so long as they are kept cool.

Matching Tackle To Bait

Rod, reel, line and hook must be matched to the bait, as well as to the size fish you hope to catch. Thus, if you're pitching unweighted dollar crabs to tarpon podding along the beaches, you're going to be limited to medium baitcasters like the Ambassadeur 7000, or medium-heavy saltwater spinning tackle, fairly flexible rods in the 7-8 foot range, and line testing around 25 pounds.

Mullet are a favorite tarpon bait, particularly along the Atlantic Coast during spring and fall mullet runs. They are hardy baits so long as they're kept in a large well with lots of raw water circulation.

On the other hand, to toss whole mullet that may weigh a pound or more, a squidder-type revolving spool reel is more the ticket. Some good ones include the Shimano Triton 200 G, Penn GLS 25 and the Daiwa SeaLine LD50H. These are necessarily mounted on a serious rod with a butt the size of a broomstick. Line testing 30 to 40 pounds is appropriate.

Live Bait Hooks

The inside of a tarpon's mouth has about as many places for a hook to catch as does the inside of a steel bucket--which is to say none.

So selecting a hook that will cut its way in is more critical with tarpon than with any other species.

One of the popular styles, proven on thousands of fish at Boca Grande Pass, is the Mustad #7690. It's a stout, short-shank model with a relatively small barb cross-section that sets readily on the 80-pound tackle used at the pass. The similar Mustad #7692 is also a favorite of many live bait anglers, in sizes from 3/0 to 6/0.

Also growing in popularity is a unique hook from the Owner Corporation known as the "Gorilla Big Game" model. This hook is made of very heavy stock, perhaps three times the thickness of normal saltwater hooks of similar size. The barb is spade-shaped, with sharpened edges and a curved tip. Though the hook looks too stout for easy hook sets, guides along the West Coast of Florida have been using it for several years now on 25-pound tackle with near-perfect results.

Again, 3/0 to 6/0 are the popular sizes, with the smaller used for shrimp, the larger for mullet and other big baits. The idea is to use a lighter hook for the more delicate offerings that have trouble toting the bigger hooks. Also, large baits such as 8- to 10-inch mullet tend to "mask" the hook with their bulk, unless you use a big one.

Anglers along the coast of Texas and Louisiana are now using the same "circle hooks" used by offshore longliners, with extraordinary success. Most report hook-up rates in excess of 80 percent, as opposed to about 60 percent with conventional hooks. Apparently the circle hooks tend to set themselves, burrowing in around the broad lips of the tarpon. (Most experts like to slightly offset the point, about 1/8 inch, to help the hook catch.)

Also good is the Gamakatsu live bait hook, another extra-stout version with a short shank. The hook has some similarity to the circle hooks used by long-liners, and tends to dig itself in without much of a hook-set on the part of the angler. It's also one of the few hooks that's sharp enough right out of the box to stick a tarpon.

Virtually all other hooks require sharpening. The quick way is with Doug Hannon's battery-powered Hook-Hone-R-- use the tip fitting sized for larger hooks. Fine-tooth metal files are also very effective, and do the job smoother and more quickly than a stone.

With the file, you can triangulate the barb, creating cutting surfaces on each edge. It takes time, but can help. Most anglers cut a flat surface on the outside of the barb area, then angle the two sides in to meet at the inside center. Work at it until the whole barb is sharpened, but don't take off more metal than necessary. A tip that's sharpened too fine may fold over on the hook set.

Some experts of late have taken to sharpening the outside edge or "back" of the barb, on the theory that this arrangement is less likely to cut it's way out of the jaw in a long battle. Many pros shorten the barb a bit on the theory that the shorter the barb is made, the less pressure it takes to sink it. Again, the fine-toothed file is used to trim away excess metal.

One hook not used for natural baits in tarpon fishing is the treble. Paradoxically, single hooks sink in much better, perhaps because all the striking force is concentrated on one point. And since you'll be releasing the fish, there's no reason to put

The squirrelfish or sand perch is a prime bait when tarpon are found in deep passes or along the beach. They're probably the most-used baitfish at Boca Grande Pass.

those extra two hooks in there to make it tougher on fish and fisherman to effect a prompt release. Speaking of release, single hooks should be bronzed, carbon steel, not stainless, because they sometimes have to be left in the fish. Bronzed hooks quickly rust out, stainless hooks don't.

Most anglers use at least five feet of 80- to 100-pound mono leader in natural bait fishing. The thickness of this mono prevents the tarpon from rubbing through with its rough jaws during a long fight, and the extra length protects against abrasion across the shoulders as the fish runs. In live-baiting at Boca Grande Pass, the guides use 12 feet of number 7 wire leader, primarily as a way of accurately controlling the depth of their baits in the snag-filled pass.

The line is connected to the leader with a stout swivel, a number 6 "solid ring" stainless or similar, and the running line is doubled with a Bimini twist, usually a fairly short one of three or four feet, unless light line is being used for a record try, in which case the maximum allowable IGFA lengths are used, 15 feet for tests up to and including 20 pounds, 30 feet for tests over 20 pounds. (Leaders of matching lengths are allowed under IGFA rules) The longer the section of double line and leader, the sooner some of this extra-strong section gets on the reel, and the sooner you can really put the power to the fish.

25

Presentation

Presentation of live baits is mostly just a matter of getting the offering where the tarpon can see it. If they're in a feeding mood and haven't seen the boat, they'll do the rest.

However, getting the bait to them at long range can sometimes present problems. If you can't whack out a 150-foot cast with a sardine, 6 or 8 feet of trailing leader and a big, bulky cork float, it might behoove you to practice until you can manage that stunt. Especially when casting to visible fish along a west coast beach, the guys who catch the most fish are the guys who can throw farthest. (Of course, 150 feet is just a warm-up to surf-casters with 12-foot Hatteras Heavers, but most boat fishermen don't want to carry these monsters.)

In general, the trick with live bait is to note the direction of travel of approaching fish, put the bait well out in front of them, and let them swim to it. You don't want to land the bait right on top of them, which sometimes flushes the school, and you don't want to pull the bait toward them, which goes against what they expect from a scared fish or crab.

If the fish are riding high in the water, often a cork will help keep the bait up in their line of travel. Most experts use natural cork, or paint a foam float brown, to avoid having tarpon snatch at it. White corks with red stripes are just as attractive to tarpon as are white surface plugs with red stripes, and they obligingly eat them.

Some anglers simply put a wrap of line around a 3-inch Styrofoam block. When the fish hits, the block is cut in half by the line and is out of the way for the battle. In these days of plastics awareness, however, that's probably not such a great program, since every bait means another chunk of foam added to those littering the world's beaches--this stuff is expected to survive both us and our grandchildren, remember.

The setting is usually three to five feet above the hook, which puts the float on the heavy leader section--a good place for it since the "jam stick" on the float might weaken lighter running line.

Dead Bait

Dead bait fishing is the least glamorous of the tarpon fishing arts, but sometimes the most effective. It's a fairly straight-forward business, anchoring the boat, putting out a half-dozen shad, mullet or similar baits on big tackle with enough weight to hold bottom, and letting them set until something happens. (A mullet head is a particularly good bait, because it's too big for catfish to swallow, too hard for crabs to ruin, but tarpon readily gulp it down.) The action can always be much improved by tossing out plenty of chopped chum of the same species you're using as bait, so that the tide carries scent to nearby fish and lures them in.

The secret to fishing dead bait is to get into an area where there are plenty of fish passing through on a regular basis, since you won't be pursuing them. Watch for plenty of rolling fish, and try to set up in their midst.

It sometimes takes an hour or more for the scent of the bait to turn on the fish, so patience is part of the game. The reels are left in free spool, with the clicker on, so that a tarpon can take off on his first run unobstructed.

Fishing dead bait is not nearly so interesting as whipping out 90 feet of fly line to a visible pod of fish, but sometimes it's the only thing that works. If you really want to catch a tarpon, keep it in mind.

The Take

Whatever the hook, the point should be completely exposed. There's no need to "hide" the hook in the bait so the fish won't know it's there. Tarpon aren't that cautious, and a buried hook will not catch many fish. The point, barb and bend have to be out there where they can snatch into the jaw, or you might as well stay home.

The exposed hook also makes it possible to strike the fish immediately on the pick-up. This is very important, because if a tarpon is allowed to run off with a bait and swallow it, chances of the fish's survival after release are greatly reduced.

A gut-hooked tarpon does not put on a tarponly battle, in any case, and that's why you're out there sweating in the August sun, isn't it?

There's no question about whether you've got a bite when a tarpon takes a live or cut bait. There might be a short bump before he catches it, but once the bait is in the fish's mouth, you'll know it. The line tightens, the rod goes down, and

27

things start to happen fast--you may wonder what you've gotten yourself into.

As soon as the fish draws the rod down, it's time to strike, setting it with all the line will take four or five times--unless, of course, you subscribe to the theory of some guides, who vow that it's best not to set the hook at all because the fish pulls the barb into itself on the first run. Probably the best approach is to evaluate each take and act accordingly--if the fish freight-trains the bait and takes off at Mach I, you won't need much of a hook set. If he takes less authoritatively or on a slack line, better crank down and let him have it, several times, with all the line will stand. Some anglers like to set a couple times after the first jump, just to re-bed the barb. You'll develop your own prejudices after you've jumped your first half dozen fish.

For what to do next, read Chapter 6--preferably before you hook the fish.

CHAPTER 4

ARTIFICIALS FOR TARPON

IT WAS A BRAVE MAN that first threw a bass plug at a tarpon.

Tarpon readily take the same small lures loved by largemouth bass, and consequently can be hooked, fought and sometimes caught on the same tackle, the ubiquitous baitcaster embodied by the Ambassadeur 5000, mounted on a stout "eye-crosser" of a worm rod.

You can do it, but it's doing it the hard way.

While you can readily hook tarpon on bass tackle, you soon begin to wish that you hadn't. The rod that seems shovel-handle-stout when jerking in a 5-pound largemouth feels more like a wet noodle when applied to the antics of an infuriated hundred-pound tarpon, especially if the fish happens to be looking at you from some altitude.

Tarpon are among the few fish that will literally look down at the fisherman, because the jumps of a big one readily take him six to eight feet into the air. When the fish adds injury to insult by sailing that mouthful of hooks back into your face at 90 miles an hour, you may decide to take up safer sports, such as sky-diving.

On the other hand, you may become irretrievably addicted, and be unable to await more of the same treatment.

The Right Tackle

You can catch tarpon on bass gear, but you'll do a lot better on something considerably more substantial. A stout,

29

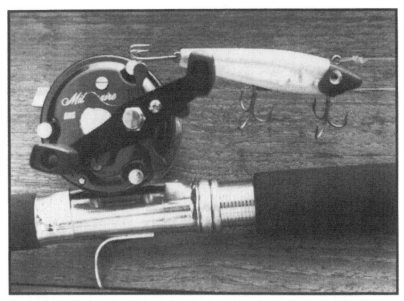

Free-spooling baitcasters mounted on stout, two-handed rods are the ticket for most plug-casting situations. Line capacity should be at least 250 yards for tackle to be used from a boat that can follow the fish, 350 yards for a pier or beach rig.

7-foot rod with a base about as thick as your index finger, tapering rapidly in the last 18 inches or so to give a fast-action tip for easy casting, is the ticket. The grip should be a two-hander, so you can reach up above the reel and really put the pressure on when you stick a horse, and the guides should be lined with one of the smooth, hard ceramics for low friction as hundreds of yards of line go ripping through.

The Ambassadeur 7000 is a hard reel to beat among the baitcasters. Penn's GTi 310 is also sturdy and long on line capacity, though it has a somewhat awkward free-spool mechanism, as do all other reels of this size excepting the Ambassadeur. Basically, you want a reel that can handle 250 yards or more of 25-pound-test.

In spincasters, Daiwa's Black Gold series is generally recognized as one of the tops, with the BG30 and the BG60 among the favored tarpon sizes. Shimano's larger "Aero" versions and the Penn 650SS and 704Z are also well-respected. Most spin-fishermen use 20 to 25 pound test.

Hand-tied jigs like this one work well for tarpon on the flats. So does the "floating" jig, a jig with a cork head, known as the "Bill Smith Lure." Twelve-Fathom Jigs in Largo, Florida, makes a commercial floating jig.

Avoid Light Lines

If you're looking for an IGFA world-record, of course you'll want to use line considerably lighter than these weights, but for general recreational angling, it makes better sense to use fairly stout string. It can take hours to land a 100-pound fish on 8-pound test, and by that time the tarpon is almost certain to die when finally released. (You may think you're going to die, as well, after such a long battle.)

Use appropriately stout tackle and you'll get the most out of the fish, yet can release it in short order so that it can fight again.

Plugging For Tarpon

One of the great pleasures in tarpon fishing is drifting a jungle river, tossing a stocky surface plug ahead of you as you wait to happen up on a school of fish.

Tarpon hit topwaters with an explosion that is probably unmatched in all of sportfishing. One mirror-calm afternoon on Charlotte Harbor, I saw a six-footer rise up from the black depths like a giant rainbow trout, make a crashing arch of a leap, and land ON TOP of my 5M MirrOlure, gulping the plug on the way down just as those cold water salmonids gulp down Mayflies. Other fish took the plug in a more conventional manner, coming from below to inhale it in a Jacuzzi-sized boil. Absolutely awesome.

It's unusual to find big fish so willing to blast topwaters, but small tarpon up to 40 pounds or so readily climb all over them, especially when they're presented in slightly murky water like that found throughout most of the Florida Everglades, as well as in much of the inshore waters along Central and South America. The noisy plugs are evidently

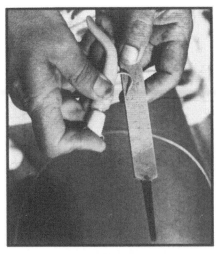

Whatever the lure, the hooks must be extremely sharp to penetrate the hard mouth of the tarpon. Many anglers triangulate the hooks, creating three cutting edges on the barb.

easy for the fish to find in the mud, and they have no hesitation about walloping them.

There are many good ones, but some of those favored by time are the 5M and 7M MirrOlure, the Bomber Long A in size 16A, the Rebel Jumpin' Minnow, Zara Spook and other fairly obnoxious floaters. Work them slow, but work them loud, and you'll draw some hair-raising strikes.

Tarpon also readily take sinking plugs, with the best choice based on the water depth. On the flats and adjoining channels, slow-sinkers like the Bagley Finger Mullet and the 52M MirrOlure are hard to beat. In water 6 to 10 feet deep, baits that sink a bit more rapidly, like the Hot Flash and Magnum Rat-L-Trap, can be effective. And for water over 10 feet deep or where there's lots of current, weighted plugs like the 65M and 72M MirrOlure are the ticket.

Whatever the plug, you'll need about 12 inches of very heavy "shock" leader (80 to 100-pound test) to protect against the tarpon's rough jaws. Yet, the plug must be allowed to move freely against the heavy line, so it's necessary to use a loop knot. This does not have to be a "hundred-percenter" because the shock leader is so much stronger than your running line. A quick, easy tie is the MirrOlure Loop Knot, which is basically two quick half-hitches.

With this leader, as in fly fishing, it's important to keep the mono straight or the plug won't work well. Some guys boil

32

Effective rods have very stout butt sections, but a fast tip to allow casting light plugs. Note how the lower section of the rod shown here has almost no bend, despite the tremendous pressure on the fish.

their mono to relax it, others stretch it, using a boat trailer winch. Whatever, it pays to get the memory completely out of the shock leader.

The shock leader can be attached directly to the running line with a Surgeon's Knot (see next chapter), if you're using 25-pound-test or stouter. This is a strong knot that's quick and easy to tie.

If you're using lighter line, add at least six feet of 30-pound-test between running line and shock leader, to act as a buffer against the sweeps of the fish's tail. Tie this into the running line, which you've doubled with a Bimini, using another Surgeon's Knot for maximum strength.

Casting to rolling fish takes a bit of calculation if you're tossing sinking lures. Often, the fish come up only long enough to gulp air, then head back near bottom as they cruise along with the school.

If you toss where they roll, you'll be behind the fish. The idea is to estimate their speed and the time it will take for your plug to sink down near bottom and lead them by that much when you make your cast. In 20 feet of water, the lead may be 50 to 80 feet with some lures, so keep this in mind when you let go.

Tarpon usually like a plug to go slowly, with short hops followed by a momentary drop. They generally don't freight-train sinking plugs as they do topwaters, and sometimes you'll feel only a slight tap when one takes hold.

When you feel that tap, it's necessary to set the hooks, fast, hard, and frequently. It helps a lot if you've installed oversized, extra-strong trebles, and of course the point has to be needle sharp. It's also a good idea to file down the barb a bit, both so that you can release the fish more easily and also so that you can drive the hooks home with less resistance.

Jigs For Tarpon

Many anglers have discovered that tarpon readily eat jigs, particularly when the fish are feeding deep or in high-current areas. Vic Dunaway, renowned editor of Florida Sportsman Magazine, was one of the pioneers of this trick at Boca Grande Pass, and it has been catching on strongly in recent seasons there.

The jigs that work best at the pass are not large, considering the size of the fish. A head weighing 1 to 1 1/2 ounces is favored, but the lure is built on an oversized hook, a 7/0 or larger in strong stock. The tail is usually a green, curly-tail plastic worm, about six inches long.

This is cast downcurrent, bounced off bottom a few times as the boat rapidly drifts toward it, and then retrieved quickly for another drop to the bottom, which varies between 40 and 70 feet away. It takes a lot of casting, but some days, the tarpon eat the jigs even better than live bait.

The same lure is known to work well in other passes, including those that feed Apalachicola Bay, in the Florida Panhandle, in late summer, and many of those running to the ocean in South Florida.

And off the coast of Louisiana, they use a big jig with a circle hook hanging on the rear to catch the monsters of late summer in water that looks murky enough to plow. Jigs and tarpon go together.

Spoons

Trolling spoons for tarpon is pretty much a lost art, but it's still effective, especially when the fish are scattered and you don't know where to start looking. Big spoons are used, 12 inches long or thereabout, pulled on heavy gear to allow authoritative hook sets. The practice still goes on in the back of Charlotte Harbor in late summer, after sundown from June through October in the Crystal River on Florida's west coast, and somewhat off the coast of Louisiana in late summer.

CHAPTER 5

TARPON ON THE FLY

"IT'S THE ULTIMATE HIGH--Catch a Tarpon On a Fly."
That's what at least one T-shirt advertises, and any angler
who has tried tarpon on the long rod is likely to agree--the
combination of giant tarpon with fly tackle is probably the
best that sportfishing has to offer.
Further, tarpon have an affinity for flies that borders on
the ridiculous. Given their enormous bulk, it seems unlikely
that they would even notice, let alone eat, a fly hardly big
enough to interest a medium-sized largemouth bass. Yet, they
can't seem to leave them alone--in the right times and places,
they seem to take flies more readily even than live baits.

Fly Rods
Well-known names in tarpon fly rods include Fenwick, the
Loomis IMX series, Sage RPL-X series, Orvis HLS series,
Scott, R.L. Winston XD models, Fisher and Graphite USA.
They range in price from $250 to $450--not cheap, by any
means.
They're expensive because there's lots of high-modulus
graphite in a 9-foot rod, and because it's tough to build a rod
with walls strong enough to stand the tremendous compression
forces of pumping a big fish, and yet flexible enough to toss a
fly line a hundred feet--they still haven't perfected the art.
Every year, anglers "blow up" or splinter high-dollar fly rods
simply by putting pressure on a tarpon. And the problem is

Tarpon on the flats show a remarkable affinity for well-presented flies. Powerful 12-weight rods are needed to do battle with the fish, and also to handle casting a long line in the constant winds.

likely to become more pronounced with the new 20-pound tippet class, though builders are rushing to build stouter sticks to handle the extra pressure. Thus, expert tarpon fly-rodders are forever engaged in the endless search for the perfect rod, and in the discussion thereof.

Twelve-weight is the standard for mature tarpon, and some anglers prefer a rod with a cork fore-grip that allows a great increase in pumping pressure when used with a fighting belt. (Others say foregrips add weight and resistance in casting, and eschew them, preferring to depend on gloves to allow a comfortable grip well up the shaft for pumping in a fish.)

Some expert anglers insist on buying rods that have not been sanded smooth, as many production rods are for cosmetic purposes. The theory is that any sanding whatever takes away a few layers of graphite fiber, and consequently weakens the rod. Under maximum stress, it may give way. Orvis, Scott and some other builders do not sand their tarpon rods.

At Homosassa, because the fish run large, some anglers opt for 13-weight rods, or seek 12's with extra butt power, to control the giants.

Fly Reels

Reels are also not cheap. They require a silky drag and lots of line capacity, plus far greater durability than fly-reels used for smaller species. Many are machined from solid aluminum,

36

A large-capacity reel with a smooth drag is critical in handling jumbo tarpon on fly tackle. Dacron backing is used rather than monofilament, because mono tends to crush the spool when rewound under pressure. The flies, tied by Capt. Bill Miller, are typical tarpon offerings. Note the long, tapered head for ease of casting.

an expensive and labor-intensive process. Tarpon reels by Fin-Nor, one of the classic builders, go for about $425 in direct or anti-reverse. Billy Pate puts his name on some excellent reels in both types, about $400 in size 11-12. The Abel 12-13 is direct drive, exceptionally light and strong, about $600. Scientific Anglers System Two 1011 has a fine drag, light weight and good durability, and is a real bargain at $160. The System 3 1112 is a bigger reel with an exceptionally smooth drag based on O rings rather than conventional disks-- it's effective and a good value. The Orvis DXR Tarpon is also a very good buy at around $375--oversized, ultra-smooth drag, bullet-proof construction, easy drag adjustment and minimal weight.

If you're right handed, you'll probably want a left-hand crank on your reel, since you'll want to use your strong right arm for pumping the rod. Most experts prefer direct drag rather than anti-reverse, because it allows them to precisely control drag pressure with their fingers on the spool.

Leaders and flies are pre-rigged, then stored in fly boxes that keep the shock leader straight. A straight leader is essential for proper fly action says Capt. Mike Locklear of Homosassa.

Fly Lines For Tarpon

Lines are as important as the rod and reel in fly fishing, with just the right taper for your casting style making a lot of difference in your distance. Some like weight-forward, some like shooting heads, which have a shorter, heavier head and very thin running line. Popular lines presently include the Orvis WF-12 F/S, which is a unique weight-forward line with a clear, sinking tip. The line effectively doubles the leader length, in terms of visibility to the fish, helps get the fly down promptly, and yet offers the easy lifting off the water of a floating line. It's expensive at around $60, but worth it for serious tarpon chasers.

The Tarpon Taper from Scientific Anglers is a very good casting line, as well. It's available in floating or sinking models. Don't get the coral color, which a lot of guides say spooks the fish--gray is better.

Scientific Anglers also makes a unique line called "Mono Core" that is virtually invisible in the water, and so slippery the guides call it "slime line"--it's pretty much the standard by which others are measured at present. It's easy for even an average caster to shoot the whole line, though picking it up

Many tarpon anglers tie their own flies. Capt. Earl Waters suggests putting an orange head on most flies so that the angler can readily see them in the water.

from the water is a bit more difficult than with floating lines. Mono Core is tough for the angler as well as fish to see, so it can present a challenge for beginning fishermen who have a hard time watching the fly itself. But many experts prefer it to any other line. It's about $45 per spool.

Cortland also makes some good tarpon lines, with a very thin running line and a short front taper to turn over heavy flies, plus shooting tapers in a variety of sink rates and colors. Prices start at a very reasonable $35.

(Whatever the line, it's a good idea to stretch it thoroughly before each day's fishing. You can do this simply by pulling it between your hands, a yard at a time. The stretching gets out any kinks, and also eliminates excessive elasticity that might make it hard to set the hook on a fish.)

You also need backing for your tarpon reel--most will hold at least 300 yards of 30-pound-test Dacron. Opt for Dacron rather than monofilament because it doesn't stretch under pressure. If you crank hard on a fish with mono, the backing will stretch just a bit with each turn of the spool, building up pressure until the spool may spread out and freeze against the frame. Dacron does not cause the problem.

Fly Patterns

Tarpon eat a wide variety of fly patterns, and most of the time they aren't fussy, though those that see lots of casts in a season can get selective on occasion.

In general, streamers tied on 2/0 to 4/0 hooks are the ticket, and for ease of casting, most are tied with a long, tapered "nose" of epoxied thread that extends about half the length of the shank, followed up with a fairly sparse dressing of hair and feathers. Total length of the fly rarely exceeds four inches.

Among the all-time favorites is the "Cockroach", a brown Florida Keys concoction that has a pair of curved feathers aft that "breath" as the fly is stripped through the water. It probably resembles a shrimp, and is the preferred fly by many experts in clear water. If you like the idea but want a bit more color, try Chico Fernandez' variation, which adds a bit of orange to the Cockroach. (Capt. Earl Waters puts a head of orange thread on all his flies, so the angler can more readily see it moving through the water.)

Attractor patterns in bright colors also catch plenty of fish, and are the flies of choice in murky water--the Everglades and much of Central America--as well as sometimes on clear flats. The yellow-and-orange Stu Apte Tarpon Fly is a standard.

Guides at Homosassa are often partial to purple, and this is a favorite pattern in "green" water situations everywhere. Chartreuse also is a good color at Homosassa.

There are also leech-type lures made of rabbit fur, that are a very good imitation of the palolo worm--great in orange or brown when the worm hatch is on in the Florida Keys. A red-and-black fly known as "Black Death" is also a keys favorite.

Leaders

The leader is critical in tarpon fishing because it is essentially made up of several pieces of mono, and each connecting knot is a potential trouble spot.

The leader has to roll the fly over at the end of the cast, which requires a stout butt section, tapering to lighter weights. It has to contain the required line-class tippet, in case you should luck into an IGFA record. And it has to finish off with a "shock" section of very heavy material to prevent chafing in the rough jaws of the tarpon.

Any serious tarpon angler needs a leader dispenser box, to keep the various strengths of leader material under control

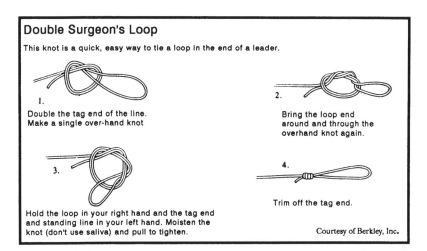

Double Surgeon's Loop

This knot is a quick, easy way to tie a loop in the end of a leader.

1.
Double the tag end of the line.
Make a single over-hand knot

2.
Bring the loop end
around and through the
overhand knot again.

3.
Hold the loop in your right hand and the tag end
and standing line in your left hand. Moisten the
knot (don't use saliva) and pull to tighten.

4.
Trim off the tag end.

Courtesy of Berkley, Inc.

and readily at hand. A pair of nailclippers, suspended around the neck on a tether, is also standard equipment for those who must build the final connection.

Most experts like a "hard" mono for leaders, one with a minimum of the flex that's important for good casting on conventional reels. Mason is the standard, but some of the high-durability monos from main-line builders are also used.

Whatever the brand, the shock leader must run perfectly straight, and guides have devised several tricks for getting the "memory" out of line that normally never forgets.

Captain Bill Miller of Tampa boils his 100-pound until it relaxes like a cooked lobster. Earl Waters of Homosassa ties his to the winch on his boat trailer, through a pulley, and then to a tree. He takes out all the stretch, lets the line stand over night, then takes out the stretch again, and so on for three days.

When the completed leaders are stored, this straightened section is held under tension in a leader box or tube, so that it does not tend to curl back to its old shape once again. The rest of the leader is wrapped in a large coil adjacent. Thus, a dozen or more leaders with flies attached are usually kept at hand.

There are several ways of building a tarpon leader, all of them involving more knots than you'll want to tie--but experience has proven the time-consuming and precise series of attachments is most dependable.

In general, most anglers like to include a loop at the tip of the fly line or the end of the butt section of leader so that the tippet, shock leader and the fly can quickly be changed without going through the whole series of knots needed, if the fly pattern is not working or if the leader is damaged. However the thing is put together, it looks like an accident in a monofilament factory, but it works for holding the power of big tarpon.

You can create the loop at the end of the line with any of several whipping-style knots, with the Nail Knot used by many expert anglers. Use a 10-inch length of 10-pound mono for the whipping to create the flyline loop, doubling the line back on itself about 2 inches. Captain Earl Waters ties three separate Nail Knots to secure the loop. Some anglers secure the mono with a touch of Crazy Glue. The finished line loop is small, no more than 1/4 inch wide.

To this, you attach the butt section of the leader, usually 40- to 50-pound test about 5 feet long, but perhaps 8 to 10 feet long if the water is very clear or the fish exceptionally spooky. A seven-times-around Uni-Knot can be used to make a loop in the butt for attachment to the fly-line loop. Tied with the extra turns, the Uni doesn't slip.

On the other end of the butt section, those who like to make their change from the butt section forward create another loop in the butt, again created with a seven-times-around Uni-Knot.

This is set aside momentarily while the class tippet is made up. Using leader material known to break at or lower than the IGFA class you're fishing (pre-testing or buying class line is essential if you're after a record), make up a 24 inch tippet section with a Bimini twist doubling the line at each end. Make the double line sections about 8-10 inches long.

Attach one doubled section to the butt loop. Double the double line and tie a Surgeon's Knot to create a loop about 3 inches long, large enough to easily slip over the fly, so that this section can be removed easily and another substituted.

To the doubled line on the other end of the tippet section, tie in your shock leader, 12 inches of 100-pound test for typical mature tarpon, maybe up to 150-pound test for Homosassa jumbos. The knot commonly used is the Albright Special, though some use the Uni-knot.

Earl Waters creates a loose figure 8 knot in the shock leader, threads the doubled line through it, draws down the figure 8 with pliers, and then throws a series of half-hitches over the shock leader and finishes off by back-wrapping over the knot.

The entire shock leader, including the knots, must not exceed 12 inches for IGFA consideration. Make yours a half-inch short, to allow for stretch during the fight.

The fly is attached to the shock tippet with a loop knot so that it swings freely, providing added action. Knots used for this are the Improved Homer Rhodes, a loop Uni-Knot with seven turns, two-wrap Hangman's or others. Some anglers prefer to snell the fly to the leader, since this creates no visible loop that might put the fish off and also assures that the fly will run straight.

And there you are--nothing to it, see?

It's possible, likely in fact, that learning to tie all these knots will take you more time than learning to fly cast. But, once learned, you can take the same pride in tying up your own leaders that a parachutist takes in packing his own 'chute--and the same responsibilities, if something goes wrong.

Casting Tips

A tarpon boat is no place to learn to cast a fly--but it's been done, plenty of times, as guides provide the basics for tyro clients. Casting a fly 50 feet or so (far enough to catch many a tarpon) is not difficult with a good instructor, and many guides are excellent.

However, you'll do a lot better if you learn how to do the job with 12-weight gear at home, practicing until it becomes instinctive, so that you don't choke when you've got a spread of hundred-pounders bearing down on you. (Everybody does choke at times, but your "choke threshold" goes up if you're confident of your casting.)

Though 50 feet will catch fish, 65 or 70 is better, and 90 is great. It takes time, practice, and usually a bit of instruction to begin hitting the end of the line, but most anglers can manage it after a few extended sessions. Interestingly, the longer casts take very little more power than the 50 footers. (As Bill Miller--one of the better instructors--points out, once you get on to it, you understand that timing gives you "effortless power, rather than powerless effort", and don't look as if you're trying to whip a horse with your flailing.)

It's often necessary to cast quickly, so guides advise the angler to get at least 20 feet of line out the tip. This is hung in a broad loop over the side of the boat, while the angler holds the fly and a large coil of leader in his left hand (assuming a right-hand caster). About 50 feet of line is dropped in large coils from the reel, spread in broad loops to one side of the casting deck, or just off the platform, if there's a lot of wind that might blow it overboard.

When fish are sighted, (wear Polarized glasses with side guards, of course, and a long-billed hat to shade them) the fly is tossed over the side, and in no more than two or three backcasts, a 70-footer is shot out. Endlessly sawing the air with repeated backcasts very often puts the fish down.

Captain Ray DeMarco suggests that his fly-rod anglers take off their shoes when they cast, so that they know instantly if line gets under their feet. The line must be kept free so that it won't hang up on the cast, and, should a fish be hooked, so that it won't tangle on the first run. You can't tell if you wear shoes--and shoes also crack the finish of some lines, ruining them in short order.

Captain Earl Waters advises his anglers to make several trial casts on stakeouts to study the effect of wind and current on the fly line. Often, these practice shots make all the difference when a school approaches.

When a school is within range, the fly is cast ahead of the pack so that it can sink down in front of the fish as they approach.

"If the fish are making shallow rolls, they're running high in the water," says Waters."If they arch high when they roll, they're swimming along bottom. Try to let your fly sink accordingly. Remember, the water may make the fish look closer than they are -- be sure to make your cast long enough."

When the fish are within 5 to 10 feet of the fly, it's drawn across their path, ideally quartering slightly away from them,

Bimini Twist

The Bimini Twist creates a long length of double line stronger than the single strand of the standing line. Most often used in offshore trolling, it is also applicable in light tackle trolling. Use these directions for tying double-line leaders of around 5 feet or less.

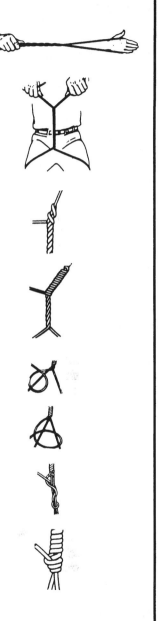

1. Measure a little more than twice the footage you'll want for the double-line leader. Bring end back to standing line and hold together. Rotate end of loop 20 times, putting twists in it.

2. Spread loop to force twists together about 10 inches below tag end. Step both feet through loop and bring it up around knees so pressure can be placed on column of twists by spreading knees.

3. With twists forced tightly together, hold standing line in one hand with tension just slightly off the vertical position. With other hand, move tag end to position at right angle to twists. Keeping tension on loop with knees, gradually ease tension of tag end so it will roll over the column of twists, beginning just below the upper twist.

4. Spread legs apart slowly to maintain pressure on loop. steer tag end into a tight spiral coil as it continues to roll over twisted line.

5. When spiral of tag end has rolled over column of twists, continue keeping knee pressure on loop and move hand which has held standing line down to grasp knot. Place finger in crotch of line where loop joins knot to prevent slippage of last turn. Take half-hitch with tag end around nearest leg of loop and pull up tight.

6. With half-hitch holding knot, release knee pressure but keep loop stretched out tight. using remaining tag end, take half-hitch around both legs of loop, but do not pull tight.

7. Make two more turns with the tag end around both legs of the loop, winding inside the bend of line formed by the loose half-hitch and toward the main knot. Pull tag end slowly, forcing the three lops to gather in a spiral.

8. When loops are pulled up nearly against main knot, tighten to lock not in place. Trim end about 1/4 inch from knot.

Courtesy DuPont Stren

45

in sharp, erratic strips of the line, 6 to 10 inches at a time by drawing it in with flicks of the left hand as the right index finger holds tension against the line and rod. Tarpon are much more likely to follow a fly that seems to be escaping, rather than one that swims toward them.

"If you have a choice, try to work the second or third fish in a school," advises Waters. "If you throw to the first fish and it turns and follows the fly to the boat, the whole school will come along with it, and if the first fish doesn't take, the whole school will see you and blow on out. If you throw to fish back in the pack, they'll peel out to chase the fly, and if they don't take you can often pick it up and pitch it back to the main school and still get one of the last fish to take."

Waters also advises selecting a fish well away from the boat, rather than one that's only 30 feet distant, if you have a choice. The fish that's too close, he notes, often sees the boat before it takes, while the distant fish has a chance to follow the fly and take before it becomes suspicious.

On daisy-chaining or circling fish, the fly is usually presented on the outside of the circle, and on the side that is rotating toward you. That way, the fly moves in the direction the fish are going and appears to be trying to get away, rather than coming head-on at them--a very unlikely thing for a baitfish or shrimp to do.

On calm days, Waters suggests throwing an "open" loop on the final forward cast, to allow the fly to waft down, rather than splatting on the surface as it does when a fast, narrow loop is thrown.

The rod is kept low, pointed at the fly as you strip, to avoid line slap on the water. If a fish follows the fly in close, most anglers crouch to keep a low profile and avoid being seen. If the fish are deep, the rod tip is thrust under water to force the fly down.

Setting The Hook

When a fish begins to follow the fly, the strips should be increased in erratic behavior, though not necessarily in speed or length. The idea is to keep the fly just ahead of the fish's nose, until she opens her mouth with the clear intent to take-- don't slow up, or she'll often turn away.

When the fly disappears or the fish flashes sideways, or when you see the mouth open and close, wait a second or two until the fish turns sideways to go back to the school before trying to set the hook. A set when the fish is headed straight at you usually results in pulling the hook free, while a set as the fish turns usually drives the barb into the jaws. Earl Waters advises picking up slack with the left hand and feeling for the weight of the fish before moving the rod at all.

"If you feel the weight, set the hook by jerking the line three or four times. Let the fish run off the slack and get in the reel and then come back hard with the rod several times too."

If you don't feel the weight, he says, keep an eye on the fish--it may not have taken, but it may not have lost interest. Perhaps a few more twitches will do the job, where if you strike too soon, the fish is gone.

Most pros like to set the hook three or four times more after the first series of jumps, just to make sure.

The Fight

If the hook goes in, the fish usually jumps immediately and takes off on a very fast, long run. Clearing the loose line off the deck, getting the fish "on the reel" is critical at this point. You have to avoid stepping on the line, feed it up in smooth coils and hope there's not a snarl. Once the line goes out the guides and the fish is into the backing, the real work begins, but at least you have a bit more time to consider your moves than in those first frantic moments.

Many anglers these days make use of a fighting belt which offers a socket just above the groin area, so that the rod butt can be rested there rather than jammed into the stomach or side, where it invariably creates long-lasting bruises. With the fighting belt, the angler can apply his right arm to the rod, usually somewhere between the grip and the first guide, and the left to the grip. This allows leveraging the fish in with the back and shoulders rather than the far weaker biceps, and is far easier for most fishermen. The left hand is quickly shifted down to take up the line gained as you lower the rod for the next pump, or it can remain on the reel, depending on personal preference.

Most pros set their mechanical drag fairly light, at about 1/3 the strength of the tippet. They apply additional drag pressure as the fish calms down after the first runs, by using finger pressure to pinch the line against the rod, and by palming the outside of the spool on direct drive reels--one of the reasons many experts prefer direct drive. In general, this extra pressure is used as the fish is pumped closer, relaxed anytime it attempts to run or jump. As with conventional tackle, the angler always bows anytime the fish jumps, to prevent its falling on a taut line.

Fly tackle presents one unusual hazard, in that the bulk of the fly line curving through the water can create excessive drag if a fish makes a long, arching run. When a fish must be followed with the outboard to prevent its cleaning the backing, it's best to follow the line at the point where it enters the water, rather than running straight toward the fish. If you go straight, the line may form such a wide arc that the water pressure will break the tippet as the fish and the boat pull on opposite ends.

You won't land every tarpon you hook on the fly, even if you do everything right. The average is probably 1 for 5, with the top anglers getting maybe 1 of 2. But you get an amazing number of strikes using the long rod, and every fish is experienced to the max. In fishing, it probably is the ultimate high.

CHAPTER 6

FIGHT TO WIN

IT'S NOT THE SIZE of the dog in the fight, but the size of the fight in the dog.

Paul Hawkins might have been the inspiration of that old saying. Paul, a well-known St. Petersburg, Fl. guide, will never play offensive lineman in the NFL. Soaking wet--and with five pounds of jigs in his pockets--he weighs maybe 150. But Hawkins can whip a tarpon bigger than he is in the time it takes many men to reel in an average-sized redfish.

Conventional wisdom is that it takes about a minute per pound to put away a tarpon. Hawkins doesn't buy it. The rawboned little guy views long battles like Woody Hayes viewed the forward pass, a situation in which one of three things is likely to happen, two of which are bad.

"You keep that fish out there long enough, and either the hook will pull or the line will break," he observes. "And, the longer you fight him, the tireder he gets and the less chance you have of releasing him successfully."

(OK, so three bad things can happen.)

Hawkins is not a man to wait around for those bad things to happen. I've watched him, on several occasions, dismast hundred-pound fish in 20 minutes or less. And he uses only 20-pound-test gear to do it.

Tampa's Bill Miller, also a noted tarpon guide, is equally adept at putting away the big ones in record time. The secret, both anglers agree, is not in brute strength, not by a long shot.

49

"You can't just out-muscle a fish," says Hawkins. "If you're out there mindlessly pulling on the rod, you're going to get into a two or three hour mess and probably kill both the fish and yourself. You have to think about what's happening and beat the fish with your head, not your biceps."

When a tarpon or any other gamefish is first hooked there are several minutes of panic when the fish first realizes that its motion is being restrained. During that period, it wildly expends energy and soon comes to a point of near-exhaustion at which it can be brought to the boat quickly.

But if the angler doesn't take advantage of this lull, many fish seem to adjust to their plight and begin to pull more steadily, at a pace they can maintain for hours.

"When you first hook a big fish," says Miller, "whether it's a tarpon, cobia, king or whatever, the only thing you can do is let him go. If you try to stop him, the line breaks and it's over."

Drag Control

During those first moments, the drag has to be set lightly--no more than 1/3 the breaking test of the line. And it may be necessary to further reduce the drag during an exceptionally long run.

You do this most easily simply by pointing the rod at the fish. The line running through the guides when the rod is high adds a bit of drag and friction, but that disappears with the rod pointed at the fish. This is a recommended course with fish that don't usually jump, such as king mackerel.

With jumpers such as tarpon, however, it's necessary to keep the rod high, so that you have a safety margin of extra line draped between the tip and the fish.

When the tarpon jumps, you immediately "bow to the king", dropping the rod tip and bending at the waist to throw a few feet of slack into the line. This is so that, if the fish falls on the line during the jump, he won't break it. It also helps prevent snatching the hook out of the fish's mouth as he rapidly shakes his head. Headshakes in the water are slowed by water pressure, but when a tarpon leaps, he can literally switch ends in mid-air, so it's necessary to reduce pressure on the leader and hooks by bowing and dropping the rod tip.

It's also a good idea, the pros agree, to avoid letting a fish get too far from the boat. As more and more line pours into

Hooked tarpon put on a spectacular battle that can last for hours. But anglers who know the tricks can shorten the fighting time, making it easier to release the fish alive.

the water, it usually forms wide loops following the changing arcs of the fish's run. These loops themselves can add a great deal of drag as they are pulled through the water--sometimes enough to cause the line to pop. This is particularly true in fly fishing because of the thick diameter of the fly line, and also because the tippet is likely to be light.

Long lengths of line are also more exposed to other misfortunes, such as snagging a crab trap float or a channel marker, or picking up weeds. So the best policy is to follow the fish with the boat, keeping it within about 150 feet or less as much as possible.

The shorter range fight also gives the angler an advantage with lines testing under 20 pounds, because it cuts down line stretch. Monofilament elongates under pressure, and this stretching can reduce the force applied at the rod considerably, making it easier on the fish, tougher on the angler.

You can apply added pressure to the drag when you need it by cupping the spool, with a spinning or fly reel, or by putting your thumb on the side of the spool, with a baitcaster.

(Avoid thumbing the line itself, because if the fish makes a sudden run, you'll get a friction burn.) Some anglers also like to run the line between thumb and index finger on the rod hand, allowing them a final fine-tuning of drag, after the first long runs are over.

Flyrod anglers frequently run the fly line between rod and index finger to control drag pressure, squeezing down when they pump the rod, easing off when the fish jumps or runs. These maneuvers are most useful when you're pumping the fish toward you, after it has settled down a bit. You thumb the spool to prevent the drag from slipping, and pump the rod toward you to gain line. Reel up what you've gained, then thumb the spool and pump again. The advantage of this over tightening the mechanical drag is that you can immediately release the pressure, if the fish decides to make a run.

Winning The Battle

After the first frantic explosions--perhaps 10 minutes into the fight--the angler can promptly begin to do a lot of damage if he handles the rod right.

"Whatever the fish wants to do, you try to prevent him from doing it," says Miller. "If he wants to turn left, you pull to the right. If he goes right, you pull left. If he goes down, pull up. The idea is to confuse the fish and wear it down quickly."

Hawkins says he also likes to use what fly-rodders call the "down and dirty", putting the rod tip down almost into the water and pulling sideways or backward on a crossing fish.

"Toward the end of a fight, this is the single most effective method," says Hawkins. "There comes a time when you actually turn the fish over, roll him on his side or maybe over on his back. When that happens, you know you've got him if you move in fast and really put on the pressure."

When the fish is about to give up, it may release a stream of bubbles, blowing out its air in a last effort to stay down. When the bubbles come up, the fish will soon follow, some guides note.

It's necessary to close the last 30 feet or so promptly when a fish is rolled, the guides say, because if you don't, it may soon recover and regain steam.

"Every fish is different," Miller notes. "Some are done the first time you roll them, and some won't give up and you have

Capt. Paul Hawkins "bows to the silver king", dropping his rod and bending at the waist to prevent a fish from falling on his taut line.

to stop them several times, literally pull them to a dead stop when they're swimming the other way the best they can."

However, even when it seems to be all over, the angler has to stay alert, the guides advise.

"A lot of fish are lost in that last 10 or 20 feet," Hawkins says. "Sometimes you think a fish is all done, and all at once he takes off and rips off a hundred feet of line and jumps at the end of it. If you're not ready and don't keep the drag loose, you'll lose him."

Here, too, the experts suggest using thumb pressure on the spool to add drag as you pump a fish the last few feet to the gaff, rather than increasing the mechanical drag. Then, if the fish lunges, you simply raise the thumb and the drag slips.

Even after the leader is in reach on a big fish, the fight may not be over. The rod man can usually relax once his partner grabs the leader and takes aim with the gaff, but not always. There are many times when a missed effort with the gaff hook inspires a flurry, and if the rod has already been set aside, it may follow fish and line into the depths.

With very large fish, tarpon, marlin and the like, there have been numerous cases of the leaderman getting jerked overboard, either through mistakenly wrapping the leader around his hands or by hanging on to the gaff too long.

The danger of this sort of thing increases the shorter the battle, because a fish brought to the boat green is likely to find explosive extra energy at gaffing.

This is all the more true in these days of catch and release, when nobody wants to make use of "kill" gaffs with flying heads attached to a rope which can be looped over a boat cleat. The smaller lip gaffs used to control fish until they can be released are generally one-handers, which don't allow the leaderman to apply full strength to the task at hand. The bottom line is to be ready for anything at the final moment, including assisting your boat partner back aboard as you feed line to a still-frisky fish.

"There are some risks in bringing in green fish, for sure," says Hawkins. "But you're giving the fish a lot better chance to survive, and you're not fighting it so long that you begin to hate what you're doing. Knowing how to put them down quick is something that every angler ought to learn."

Conditioning

Taking on a big tarpon on light tackle takes some physical strength and endurance, no doubt about it. Even a short, 20-minute battle where you do everything right and the fish gives up promptly will leave you gasping and your arms shaky. If you hook a tough fish that fights on, hour after hour, you need to be in good shape to stand it.

Bicep exercises are particularly helpful, because you lift the rod hundreds of times during a long fight. Ten-pound dumbbells are good to start out with if you've been a bit lax about exercising of late. Start about six weeks before tarpon season and you'll be ready for a sustained battle.

It's a good idea to do some running, too, at least a mile daily, to build up your overall endurance. Spending several hours battling a big fish on a calm afternoon of 95-degree weather is tough, and you'll need all the conditioning you have time for.

Avoid drinking beer or other alcoholic beverages on the water, since they slow your reflexes and pull water out of your system. Instead, drink plenty of cool water, before, during and after the catch. If you feel yourself getting overheated, have your partner douse you with a couple buckets of water.

Finally, unless you do a lot of manual work and have tough hands, wear light cotton gloves. Otherwise, the rod grips and reel handle will blister your hands in a long fight.

Al Pflueger, Jr., gives a big Homosassa tarpon the "down and dirty" in order to pull the fish off balance. Pflueger was one of the originators of this trick and many others in fly fishing for tarpon.

Gaffing Techniques, Safety

The final moments of battle are not without a bit of danger. Going hand-to-hand with a wild fish that's bigger than you are seems an awesome task on first approach, and it can result in problems for the careless.

Most pros wear gloves and grasp the 100-pound-test shock leader in their left hand, using it to guide the fish the last few feet to boatside. The leader is never wrapped around the hand, so that it can be released promptly if the fish lunges.

The gaff is a small one, with a bite of about 2 1/2 to 3 inches. The handle is short, usually under a foot long. Most anglers use a retainer cord on the gaff to prevent its loss. But the looped cord is placed over the thumb, then brought around behind the hand before the handle is grasped, so that the cord can be shaken off if a strong fish gets wild.

The gaff is eased under the jaw, slightly to one side of the tip, and brought up in a smooth, firm pull. There's usually a slight flurry at this point, requiring a firm grip on the gaff.

Captain Earl Waters of Homosassa likes to slip the gaff inside the tarpon's mouth and come out, on the theory that this causes less damage to the mouth. Both approaches work.

With tired fish under 60 pounds, some anglers omit the gaff all together, instead simply hanging on to the jaw with both gloved hands. Once the fish settles down, the hook can be removed with longnose pliers, and the tarpon can be hoisted part way out of the water for a photo.

Live Release

There's no reason to keep a tarpon these days, unless you suspect a particular fish may be a line-class record. In Florida, the Marine Fisheries Commission has imposed a $50 tag that's needed to kill a tarpon, a program instituted specifically to stop wanton killing of fish for dockside photos.

Nowadays, all mounts are done from fiberglass molds, which are lighter, far more durable and hold color better than skin mounts. In the bad old days, some unscrupulous guides encouraged anglers to kill their fish "for mounting," when in fact the kill was made to lock the fisherman into paying for a mount--and in turn getting the guide a commission from the taxidermist.

All it takes for a mount is a quick measurement of the fish, plus a photo to act as a guide to the coloration from a specific locale. It's not necessary to lift the fish all the way into the boat for the measurement, and it is not good for their survival to do so.

To successfully release a tarpon alive, it's essential to get the fish back to swimming promptly. It's often a two-man operation, with one angler holding the fish's head steady with the lip gaff, the other removing the hook. With artificials and flies, the hook can usually be retrieved with long-nosed pliers. If the hook is buried deep, as it may be in fishing natural baits, the leader should be cut as close to the hook as possible. (Avoid using stainless steel hooks, which won't corrode away in this situation. "Bronzed" or tinned hooks disappear fairly rapidly in saltwater, and will cause no permanent harm in most fish.)

Once the hook is out, the boat is moved slowly through the water via push pole or trolling motor while the angler holds the fish alongside the boat, mouth partly open so that water flows over its gills. After a few minutes of this, most fish will start to swim on their own and try to shake loose.

That's the signal to say goodbye, taking them by the tail and pushing them out and down, so that they get a running start.

Treated this way, the vast majority of tarpon survive to fight another day. In a fish that may live more than 50 years, giving back a life truly amounts to something--you may literally be releasing a fish that will be caught by your son, or grandson.

THE FLORIDA KEYS AND FLORIDA BAY

THE FLORIDA KEYS are Grand Central Station for both tarpon and tarpon anglers, with huge numbers of the bright fish prowling the vast flats from April through June each year, and moderate numbers available year around. Most of the masters of light-tackle sight fishing for tarpon perfected their craft here, and many are resident guides.

Where to begin, in a fishery that spreads out through 150 miles of shimmering, air-clear flats veined with emerald channels and surrounded by a blue-green sea? At the beginning of the year, perhaps, and for that one goes to Key West, the last of the bridge-connected keys, to fish Key West Harbor.

Key West And The Lower Keys

From December through March and sometimes later, remarkable numbers of tarpon stack up in the deep water of the harbor in downtown Key West. In fact, tarpon are caught there year around, but it's the ONLY spot that consistently produces in winter, and thus a magnet for first-of-the-year tarpon anglers. It's also an ace-in-the-hole, in any month, when tarpon on the flats won't cooperate.

This is not classic tarpon fishing. The water is deep and often murky due to ship traffic and mud stirred by winter winds on the adjacent flats, but the tarpon are usually abundant and fairly cooperative. Most catches are made on 30- to 40-

r, soaking a crab, mojarra, jumbo shrimp or other on bottom from an anchored boat, all within sight of uise ship docks and the tourist-jammed streets of ntown. Chumming with cut fish helps bring fish to the oat on tide flows.

Key West has become sort of a Martha's Vineyard south in recent years. One hotel that caters to anglers is Pelican Landing on Garrison Bight. The facility was built by anglers, and has everything you'd want, including large, walk-in coolers for edible fish, excellent small boat docks just a short walk from the public launch ramp, and excellent motel/condo accommodations--though the rates, like everywhere else in Key West, have gotten fairly steep. If you don't stay at Pelican Landing, it's wiser to find a room up the Keys, where rates are better and you can find a place to park your boat trailer.

When water temperatures reach 70 to 75 degrees, the tarpon that winter in the harbor and on the offshore reefs come to the flats in large schools, and traditional sight-fishing begins. They usually show on the slightly warmer Gulf flats in April, following on the Atlantic side in May.

There are a lot of likely areas around Key West, including the edges of the main ship channel, particularly early in the morning before there's a lot of boat traffic. Northwest Channel is also a travel route for fish, and worth checking along the edges where the water turns from murky green to clear. The edges of the bank around Cotrell Key, visible from this channel, are also likely. (Good permit spot, too.)

Also productive at times according to Capt. Harlan Franklin, a Key West resident and one of the best in that area, are the finger channels which run around Boca Grande Key, and the six-foot-deep basin north of the key. (The main Boca Grande Channel is over 20 feet deep, and is a good low-tide spot much of the year.) The Marquesas Keys also have fish with some frequency on the outside flats, and you generally won't see a lot of tarpon fishermen this far out, so it's a good weekend spot.

Headed back toward Key West on the Atlantic side of the flats, all the edges are likely. Pay particular attention to the occasional finger channel, excellent spots on falling water. Garrison Bight Basin, on the north side of Key West and just

The Florida Keys are Mecca to tarpon anglers, with more fish and more flats than any other area. The clear water makes sight fishing easy.

outside the Garrison Bight harbor, is also a good gathering spot for fish.

Further up the keys, there's a Y channel spreading on either side of Tarpon Belly Key, about due north of Cudjoe Key on the land-route, that often holds fish in cool weather. Access here is via marinas at Sugarloaf Key. (Follow the marked channel carefully if you're not familiar with techniques of running the flats.)

At Big Pine Key, Spanish Harbor Channel offers great fishing on the south side where local fish camps dump their carcasses. Nearby Bahia Honda Channel is one of the famed spots for spring live bait fishing, and there's a nice state campground with boat basin adjacent. Similarly productive is the span of Seven Mile Bridge, just south of Marathon, which is broken into at least five deep channels by the keys and flats that make up the spine of the islands.

The Middle And Upper Keys

Marathon is the fishing center in the middle keys, with abundant accommodations, guides and launch ramps. In the upper keys, Islamorada is the jumping off spot for most flats expeditions, though some headed for the back country of Florida Bay leave from Tavernier.

All the larger bridges spanning water at least 10 feet deep hold tarpon in this area, with the action usually best after dark. The adjoining flats are good places for a newcomer to drift along the edges, looking for stragglers in daylight hours.

61

In general, the flats expand vastly from Marathon northward, forming the big, shallow bay (Florida Bay) between the Keys and the Everglades. Dotting this bay, which averages maybe 8 feet deep, are numerous "banks" or sandbars that don't quite make it through the surface to become islands. Tarpon seem to home in on these areas as feeding and travel routes. Some of them are big, like Buchanan Key Banks, and some are small, like Bamboo Banks, but all hold tarpon at times. Nine-Mile Bank, Rabbit Key Bank and Loggerhead Bank are also noted tarpon stake-outs.

One of the nice things about the upper and middle keys is that, once you get away from the short sections of shallow flats within a mile of the keys themselves, you can run along fairly steadily to your objective bank in water that's deep enough not to worry the backcountry beginner--not so in the many basins and flats of the lower keys, where you can be in six feet of water one instant and six inches the next, even though it may be six miles to the nearest island. However, targeting the distant banks here takes a bit of navigational skill and the ability to use a compass, or alternatively a LORAN and LORAN-designated chart.

Fishing the banks is a popular technique, and you'll generally have company. To avoid ruining the fishing for others, follow the accepted routine, which is to stake-out with your push pole at the edge of the bank, in an area where you can oversee a length of the white sand that makes up along most banks. You sit there and wait for the fish to come to you on tide flows. Which tide flows? That's what you pay the guide $350 a day to know--it takes a lot of time on the water to learn when the tarpon go where.

If the stake-out routine doesn't work, you can often find tarpon by drifting the deeper basins adjacent the banks, casting to rolling fish. While fly tackle is the weapon of choice on the banks, plug gear is better in the basins because a lot of it is blind casting.

Bridge Fishing

Every deep-water bridge between the mainland and Key West has some tarpon in spring, summer and fall, and some are jammed with them. Most fish caught around the bridges

This battle took place not far from Stock Island during a palolo worm hatch. When the time is right, thousands of the red-brown worms emerge, stimulating an incredible tarpon feeding frenzy.

are caught from boats, but many of the spans have catwalks, and shorebound anglers often tangle with the silver giants-- though not so often do they land them.

Fishing is always best around the bridges after dark. You can quickly tell if there are fish around a given bridge by simply listening quietly for a few minutes. If the fish are there, you'll hear incredible explosions next to the pilings as they blast mullet, shrimp and other goodies flowing through with the tide.

Naturally, offering live baits like the natural stuff is most effective. To have a chance of landing a fish from the catwalks, you need heavy gear, 80-pound line and a broomstick of a rod. With this, you troll the live bait along the pilings on both the uptide and downtide sides, letting it swim with the flow, sometimes adding weight to get it down near bottom, sometimes free-lining it at the surface.

You can also hook plenty of tarpon on plug gear in the 25-pound range, though you probably won't land any. Cast parallel to the bridge, into the shadow, and work the plug as it sweeps in an arc downtide. The 65M MirrOlure is a good plug for this, but be sure to crunch down all the barbs so the fish can throw it after he breaks your line. Bucktail jigs in 1/2 to 1 ounce sizes also do well in this fishing.

Best known bridges include Channel 2, Channel 5, Seven Mile and Bahia Honda, but there are numerous others that also produce.

The Worm Hatch

The Keys are also home to a remarkable phenomenon when tarpon go on an incredible feeding binge that makes them appear brainless as rampaging bluefish--the annual "worm hatch." A small, eel-like critter known as the palolo worm lives in the limerock bottom of much of the keys. Sometime in May or June of most years, the worms come out in millions to spawn, and when they do, the tarpon go nuts, grabbing anything that looks remotely like the orange-brown wigglers.

Experts say the hatch occurs on the lowest evening tides of May and June, which would generally make the prime time around either the new or full moons in those months. The action goes on for about three days.

The fish bite everywhere there are worms, but one of the classic spots is a bar south of Bahia Honda Key, known to locals as the "Worm Bar".

I've also had great fishing on the north side of Stock Island, near Key West, and on several of the Atlantic side flats around Marathon.

When the hatch is on, the best fly is an orange/brown streamer. The best spinning/baitcasting offering is a rootbeer colored plastic jig with a swimmer tail, rigged with a minimum of weight on a 5/0 hook. Either bait is worked slowly, with slight twitches.

Unfortunately, the worm hatch is not totally predictable, and many anglers return year after year in the prime months without ever hitting prime time. But when it's right, you won't forget it. I once hit that peak with Capt. Harlan Franklin, and have never seen the match before or since. We jumped maybe 30 fish in a day, and saw well over a thousand. There was rarely five minutes when we were not casting to or fighting tarpon-- truly awesome!

CHAPTER 8

EVERGLADES TARPON

FLAMINGO, CHOKOLOSKEE, Port of The Islands and Marco Island are the jumping-off spots for fishing the vast watery wilderness that is the Florida Everglades. There are hundreds of good tarpon spots throughout, with the big fish usually found on the outside, the juveniles up the countless creeks, inside the hidden mangrove bays, and in the jungle rivers. Tarpon action gets dependable in March, and peaks in April, May and June. Fish are around through October on the outside, and up the rivers all year.

Flamingo

Starting at Flamingo (an excellent place to start, with outstanding launch facilities and a good tackle shop) there's good fishing on the outside at Sandy Key Basin, and at East Cape, Middle Cape and Northwest Cape along the sandy beaches that make up Cape Sable. There are a number of dug canals coming out of the backcountry in this area, and these, too, are good spots, particularly on falling water, as are Little Sable and Big Sable creeks. On the inside, the Joe River is often good, though hard to fish on weekends.

Ponce de Leon Bay, created by the outflow of the Shark and Little Shark Rivers, often has some fish, as do the lower reaches of the Harney, Broad, Rodgers and Lostman's, as you progress northwest. The bays and adjacent points of each of these flows are also likely places to check for rolling fish. Again, falling water is the best time to look, as the flow pulls bait out of the backcountry.

Chokoloskee

Fishing out of Chokoloskee, the waters around Pavilion Key and Rabbit Key sometimes produce, and on outgoing water Rabbit Key Pass, Indian Key Pass, West Pass and Fakahatchee Pass, all in the Ten Thousand Islands area, are likely.

Also productive here is the Faka Union River, including the channelized section which leads to Port of the Islands Resort. The resort caters to fishermen, with excellent docks, a good baitshop, and plenty of free advice, as well as good rooms close to the docks. (A three-mile idle zone protects the abundant manatees here--but you can sometimes catch tarpon and snook by towing a big diving plug through the zone).

Marco

In the Marco area, good locations are Cape Romano, the outside waters of Coon Key pass, Morgan Beach, Caxambas Pass, and the beach along Marco Island in late summer.

There are also often baby tarpon in the canals that parallel the old Marco road, and in many of the backcountry bays nearby.

Everglades Techniques

In general, most of this country is best for fishing natural baits or plug-casting, rather than fly fishing, because the blackwater rivers and the murky green of the bays allow little sight casting. If you move out into the basins and banks of Florida Bay, you again find clear water and visible tarpon, but in close, fly casting is going about it the hard way.

In general, you fish 'em where you see 'em in the Everglades, stopping to cast where ever rolling fish are spotted. At times, up the creeks in fall, you'll come on schools of dozens of 5 to 20 pound fish, rolling and cavorting in little flowages barely wide enough to hold them. (Not so often these days, though, as a decade back. Some, including many members of the Florida Keys Guides' Association, are concerned that the reduction of small fish may bode ill for the future in this area.)

The 52M MirrOlure is a good bet for much of this fishing, as is a 1/4 to 1/2 ounce Cotee, 12-Fathom or Bubba jig with a

Many small tarpon are caught in the murky creeks of the Everglades, a great tarpon nursery. They readily take small topwater plugs as well as sinking lures and jigs.

gold-flake swimmer tail. They also hit topwaters like the Zara Spook with vigor. In the deeper passes with strong current, heavier sinking lures like the Hot Flash, 65 M MirrOlure and similars do the job. (Bend down the barbs on the treble hooks to make it easier to release the fish unharmed)

In general, tarpon fishing is pretty good and sometimes great throughout the warm months in the Everglades, even though it's not quite as productive as some other areas. A big draw is that you might catch a tarpon on one cast, and a snook, redfish or trout on the next. It's wonderful mixed bag fishing.

Back Country Cautions

The one caveat here is that you must always carry a chart and watch it closely where ever you go, because the area has endless unmarked flats and shoals, and you can't see them in the murky water.

It is also extremely easy to get lost if you go poking back into the jungle rivers, and the Glades is not a place you would want to overnight during mosquito weather. When the sun goes down, you can literally hear them, in the millions, beginning to hum as they rise out of the mangroves! Even in

Big tarpon are most abundant in the Everglades in April, May and June, but some remain on the outside through October, and smaller fish are caught up the rivers all winter.

daylight hours, they're around, as are the no-see-ums, tiny biting gnats. You need a high-DEET repellent for the mosquitoes--but not over 30 percent according to recent health studies. One remedy is to use a mesh suit like that made by Shoo-Bug. You saturate the suit with hundred-proof DEET, rather than putting it directly on your skin. The suits also have head nets, which you'll want if you're ever out there making a few last casts after sundown.

You also need Avon Skin-So-Soft to keep the gnats away-- they are not bothered by DEET, but can't stand the skin oil for some reason. It makes you smell less like a fisherman, too.

It's possible to camp overnight in the Glades in winter, on neat little wooden platforms (complete with outhouse) set up by the park service. This can make a nice outing so long as it stays cool enough to keep the bugs down. Just be sure to store every scrap of food in tight-fitting metal containers, because there are hordes of camper-conditioned racoons around, and they will make a shambles of any unguarded chow in short order. (Don't stow food in your tent, either--the little buggers chew right through while you're off fishing.)

The backcountry is not nearly so remote as it was 20 years ago, because a lot more anglers fish it these days, but there are still areas where you can go all day without seeing another boat. Take a bit of care, anytime you get off the beaten path, and you can have a great backcountry outing, tangle with some tarpon, and come home unscathed.

CHAPTER 9

HOMOSASSA GIANTS

FOR REASONS KNOWN only to themselves, each year in late April, schools of very large tarpon gather in the clear, shallow flats between Bayport and Crystal River, Florida, a 40-mile stretch of shoals where the depth increases at only about one foot per mile from shore.

The three largest tarpon ever taken on the fly were caught here: the new 20-pound tippet class in 1991 by guide Al Dopirak and his angler Tom Evans with a 180 pounder, the 16-pound tippet class by famed international angler Billy Pate with a 188-pounder caught in 1982, and the 12-pound tippet class by Dan Malzone with a 167-pounder caught in 1986. Many larger fish have been seen and some hooked, but no one thus far has been able to take the fabled 200-pounder on the long rod.

That doesn't stop dozens of tarpon addicts from returning year after year for the attempt, and stories of the "Big Mamoo" are legend. Al Dopirak, one of the most respected of the guides who ply these waters, believes he has seen at least one fish there in excess of 230 pounds--this from a man who routinely boats better than a hundred Homosassa giants each season.

The sleepy fishing village of Homosassa is headquarters for the gathering of guides and world-class anglers. Most of the guides come in from the Florida Keys, where they spend

The Homosassa flats are noted as THE spot for giant tarpon on the fly. The deep, broad flats offer an excellent feeding area for the giants, and the clear water makes fly fishing possible.

the rest of the year chasing more abundant but not so big tarpon, and the anglers come from all over the planet.

The fish arrive the last two weeks of April, or the first of May, and remain in good numbers until the afternoon rains begin, usually by the second week of June. Sometimes, they stay longer, as late as the Fourth of July. It's likely that the fish head offshore to spawn after the long foreplay at Homosassa, where they are continuously seen forming "daisy chains", nose-to-tail circles like circus elephants. (Many of the guides believe that at least some spawning takes place here, since they have seen chaining fish release milt and eggs.)

They gather in water from four to 10 feet deep, with individual schools usually numbering from six to a dozen. Some years the fish are there in remarkable numbers, others they are hard to find. The past few seasons have been slow, prompting concerns among anglers that the fish may be reacting to excessive pressure on the limited area, where up to 40 flats boats can sometimes be seen seeking the schools.

Seasonal vagaries may also be the cause, however. When I lived at Homosassa 20 years ago--before the tarpon run had

Capt. Ray DeMarco looks for just the right fly near Pine Island, a jumping-off spot for reaching the prime tarpon flats south of Homosassa Bay.

been "discovered" by the outside world. Some seasons the fish were around in incredible abundance; it was common to see 500 or more on a tide. Other years, they were tough to find in any numbers. (The ones you found were dumber in those days, though--just about every fish offered a lure took it.)

The secret slowly leaked out, though for years the only "outsiders" were guys like Carl Navarre of Cheeca Lodge and author/film maker Stu Apte--holder of six world fly-rod records over the years. Word broke big when "Sports Illustrated" came to town to do a story on Stu's pursuit of a 200-pounder on the fly, and things haven't been the same on the flats since.

In any case, when the fish are in, the main body seems to settle in loosely-grouped schools into a fairly small area, perhaps three miles wide and five to 10 miles long. The habitat on either side of this area is identical, but for some reason most of the fish will be found somewhere in that limited zone, day after day, throughout the two-month season.

Locating the right area to fish is a matter of running and looking early in the season. Some entrepreneurs rent small planes or helicopters and fly over the area, giving them a leg up on the competition, because it's very easy to spot the fish from above when the sun is high and the seas calm.

Quiet, Please

After the pattern is established, however--usually by the end of the first week of May--running an outboard in the area

71

where the fish are gathered is likely to draw the wrath of the assembled guides and expert anglers on the flats. The fish are incredibly nervous about boat traffic, and sometimes an outboard passing a quarter-mile away can send them off toward the horizon, or at least make them too nervous to take a fly or plug.

For those with minimal experience, the routine is simply to run the outside edge of the flats, in water about 10 feet deep, looking for the loose collection of flats boats that will mark the prime fishing area.

When you reach the promised land, you motor in a very broad arc around the other boats, setting yourself for a downwind drift at least a half-mile from the fleet, and shut off the outboard.

The boat is then poled or moved by electric trolling motor through the alleged hotspot while everybody keeps an eye peeled for rolling fish, the brief flip of a broad tail, or the spread of dark green torpedoes that means tarpon close at hand.

When you can, it's best to set up to drift downwind and with the sun at your back. This makes it easiest to move the boat into range of fish ahead, makes for an easier, downwind cast, and gives you the best visibility into the water.

(Of course, per Murphy's law, the fish will frequently show up on the upwind, uptide side of the boat, often rolling directly into the sun. Such is life.)

As you complete a drift--no fish ahead, and no boats, either, indicating that you're out of the active zone--keep right on poling or drifting until you're a good quarter-mile from the nearest boat before starting your outboard. That way, you won't ruin the fishing for somebody else. Hopefully, everyone else will show you the same courtesy.

Spotting The Fish

The trick to success at Homosassa is learning to see fish at considerable distances, and in considerable depths. It's often necessary to travel hundreds of yards, trolling motors on high and leaning hard on the push pole, to cut off a traveling school of fish. If you can't see them at 300 yards or more, you'll miss a lot of opportunities.

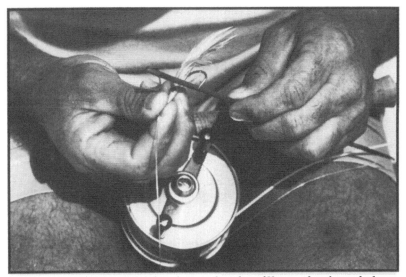

Homosassa anglers use slightly heavier gear than that of Keys anglers due to the larger average size of the fish. Many depend on flies tied on 4/0 to 5/0 hooks, and prefer 150-pound-test for shock leader rather than the 80-100 pound test used elsewhere.

It's also necessary to pick them out over a gray-green turtle-grass bottom in 10 feet of water, no easy task even for a seasoned guide. The higher above the surface you can get, the better your odds of seeing them, so the guy on the poling tower is usually the primary spotter. Some guys like to mount casting platforms or big ice chests on the bow, so the caster has plenty of elevation, too. Often, the clue you're looking for may be subtle, a quick green flash, a rising trail of bubbles, or a glimpse of shadow as the fish passes over a white sand patch. It's not easy, and most anglers miss more than they see in a day on the water.

One way to improve your odds is to locate fish over sandy or broken bottom, where it's far easier to pick them out. A vast area of white sand off Pine Island, known as "Oklahoma" by the guides, is famed for this. When the fish are in that area, it's very easy to locate them and everybody gets plenty of shots. But mostly, they are found over dark, grassy bottoms where seeing them is part skill, part skullduggery.

A Homosassa "Big Mamoo" gets airborne for Al Pflueger, Jr..

Where To Fish

In recent years, most of the fish have been caught south of Chassahowitzka Point, the long chain of mangrove and limerock islands that splits Homosassa Bay from the outflow of the Chassahowitzka River.

About a mile off the mouth of the Chassahowitzka is a noted tarpon spot known as "Black Rock Hole". It's a hole about 10 feet deep, surrounded by grass flats from 3 to 5 feet deep. On low water, tarpon frequently gather in the hole. It's also a last-chance spot, where fish can sometimes be located when they seem absent everywhere else according to captains Earl Waters and Mike Locklear, both Homosassa residents who keep very close tabs on the tarpon.

There's usually a lot of grass drifting over the hole, and crabs hide in the grass. Tarpon surface regularly to pick them off, revealing their location. The grass can make it tough to fish an artificial, but if you can find open spots, the tarpon will often take. For live bait anglers, a dollar-sized blue crab draws quick action here.

Chassahowitzka Point itself was a famed tarpon area in years past, and it still has a good showing of fish at times. Anglers often stake out on the broken limerock bottom about

Billy Pate (right) is one of the world's best known fly fishermen. His 188-pounder taken at Homosassa with guide Hal Chittum is the current IGFA 16-pound-tippet class record, and is the largest tarpon ever landed on a fly. (Photo courtesy of Riverside Villas.)

100 yards off the point on rising water, watching both inshore and offshore for passing fish.

Further north, the flats off St. Martin's Keys, on the north side of Homosassa Bay, can be very good in late June, before the scallopers arrive by the hundreds on July 1. The nice thing about fishing here is that you'll often have it to yourself, because there are fewer pods of fish than usually seen further south. But, the ones that are there will hit, which can't always be said of the hard-pressed fish at Oklahoma and other well-known areas.

Tarpon also show up in good numbers between the oyster reefs in Crystal Bay, on the north side of St. Martin's Keys. The problem in this area is that the water is frequently tannin-stained, making it difficult to see fish that are not rolling on top. However, the fish you do find are very likely to be "happy" fish, lazing along, willing to eat, since almost no tarpon boats come this far north from Homosassa.

Fishing The Rivers

Though the flats crowd leaves at the end of June, there are still plenty of tarpon around the Homosassa area throughout the dog days of summer. Fish are rare on the flats, but loads of them move into the spring-fed Homosassa and Crystal rivers, settling into the deep holes to feed on the abundant blue crabs and mullet.

You can locate river tarpon by slowly cruising the deeper areas, watching for rolling fish. When a school is sighted you can either drift and cast fast-sinking plugs like the Hot Flash or the 65-M MirrOlure, or you can anchor and put out a spread of cut mullet baits. The latter is generally the most effective technique, and it's a laid-back, relaxing way to enjoy a summer afternoon. The baits are fished on 40-pound tackle, with two or three ounces of weight to hold bottom against the tide. It's a good practice to use soft copper wire to attach the lead to the swivel at the leader connection, so that it flies free at the first jump.

A single 5/0 to 7/0 hook, carefully honed, is the ticket for consistent hook-ups. (Don't let the fish run off much after the pick-up, or you may gut-hook it and make live release impossible. Just let the fish take up the slack and draw the rod down, then set with all you've got.)

The action is best early and late on weekdays, when boat traffic is minimal. It's also very good after dark.

You can also catch tarpon in the Crystal River by slow-trolling spoons five to 10 inches long in the lower sections of the river after dark. It takes 50-pound tackle to set the hook and control the fish, but action can be explosive at times.

The river tarpon are not the giants of spring, with the average fish going 50 to 70 pounds, but there are lots of them and they extend the tarpon angler's season by several months. Fishing remains good into October most years, and some fish stay all winter in the spring-fed waters.

CHAPTER 10

BOCA GRANDE PASS

BOCA GRANDE is a trip.
Even if you don't go tarpon fishing.
The tiny, historic--and now very wealthy--town at the tip of the tiny island (about 90 miles south of Tampa) comes alive for the spring season, May and June and half of July, when the tarpon come back to Boca Grande Pass.

During this brief flurry, roads that are usually empty become busy, the shops fill up, and there are waiting lines at every restaurant. Fishing goes on day and night, with the action often best after sundown, when the lights from dozens of boats bobbing in the pass create a glow that looks like a miniature city, gliding slowly through the night.

Tarpon guides make three-fourths of their yearly income during the period, sometimes taking three charters a day and collecting over $1,000 in a 24-hour period. (They also occasionally pass out on the docks from lack of sleep!)

Fishing in the clustered fleet, you may see anybody from United States Senators to rock stars to NFL quarterbacks, all staring intently at their rod tips, listening closely to the captain's commands of "green on the tip" or "red on the reel".

It's a unique gathering, caused by a unique gathering of fish. No where else on Earth do tarpon congregate in such numbers in such a confined area as in this mile-wide pass.

Officers of the Boca Grande Fishing Guides Association estimate that in a good year, over 5,000 fish are caught and released during the 80-day season! Tarpon fishing has been a major industry here for over a hundred years, back to the days around the turn of the century when necktied gentlemen and their oarsmen were towed out to the pass in long canoes, and did battle by harpooning the fish, then going off for a Nantucket sleigh ride as the tarpon headed for the Gulf.

Literally thousands of mature silver kings jam themselves like giant sardines into this emerald-green throat of Charlotte Harbor, feeding heavily as they prepare for their offshore migration to spawn.

It's not uncommon to see schools of 50 to 100 fish sporting on top, and sometimes you may see a half-dozen or more schools of such size surfacing at once.

A chart recorder image of the 72-foot-deep "Lighthouse Hole", the deepest section of the mile-wide pass, is often black from bottom to top with the curved marks indicating tarpon shoulder-to-shoulder and nose-to-tail.

Tackle For "The Grand Pass"

Most tarpon are caught on live bait at the pass. According to Captain Jon Zorian, the favorites are mutton minnows and squirrel fish during the day, "pass crabs" or "dollar crabs" at night. The latter are small crabs about the size of a silver dollar, which flow out of the back country of Charlotte Harbor in incredible numbers during the spring tarpon run--and in fact may be the reason for its existence.

Scientists studying stomach contents of fish taken at the pass report every one of them is stuffed with the crabs. (Crabs and other live baits are usually available at Miller's Marina, a few miles north of the pass--follow the first set of channel markers and turn left at the Y. Whiddens Marina, adjacent Miller's, also has live bait, and is one of the more picturesque old structures left on the island.)

Live jumbo shrimp are also a good bait. Some of the guides depend on them in May, particularly during slack tide periods when the fish refuse all other baits.

Boca Grande and the famed "Lighthouse Hole" may offer the world's most productive tarpon fishing. The pass, at the mouth of Charlotte Harbor, has been a tarpon-fishing center for more than 100 years.

Most guides fish 80-pound-test Dacron on 30- to 50-pound-class tackle, primarily Penn International reels and stout, 6 to 7 foot roller-guide rods. The heavy Dacron does not stretch on hook sets, and has the power to control the fish amidst the heavy boat traffic. The "undersized" reels are used because they are lighter and easier to handle than 80's, and because vast line capacity is not necessary for tarpon in the pass, which rarely get more than 200 yards from the boat.

Captain Jon Zorian's favorite rigging approximates that used by most skippers in the pass--Zorian is quick to credit those who taught him, including Babe Darna, Cappy and Lamar Joiner, Freddy Futch and others of the 45-member Guides Association.

The line is tied into a heavy swivel, a number 5 brass or similar, and the leader, 12 feet of Number 7 wire, is connected to the swivel with a haywire twist. The wire is preferred to mono, even though tarpon have no teeth, because its density keeps it closer to the bottom of the pass. Mono leaders tend to "balloon" upward in the four- to six-knot current common on peak tide flows.

The weight, anywhere from 2 to 8 ounces depending on current, is attached to the swivel with a few wraps of light copper wire. When a tarpon jumps, the weight is usually thrown clear, so that it doesn't act as a bolo to jerk the hook from the fish's mouth. (Think of all the lead weights that must litter the bottom of the pass, given a hundred years of this!)

Most guides use 5/0 forged Mustad hooks, style 7690, file-sharpened for instant penetration. Gamakatsu live bait hooks are also becoming popular--their semi-circular form seems to consistently hook and hold, particularly if fishing live crabs. Boca Grande guides stitch bits of colored yarn into their line to act as markers for the length of line to be let out to keep the bait very close to bottom, but not close enough to snag the jumbles of rocks. A bit of green yarn is inserted at 42 feet, a bit of red at 60 feet. Added to the 12-foot leader length, this makes just the right total for fishing either the shallower ledges or the 72-foot maximum depth. The skipper controls the depths of the bait by instructing the client to put "green on the tip", "green on the reel" or "red on the tip", "red on the reel." It's a handy shorthand that avoids most snags, yet keeps the bait in the strike zone most of the time.

Hooking Boca Grande Tarpon

Curiously, most guides don't bother to fish for tarpon where they see them rolling. The theory is that the rollers are "playing" or going through some sort of pre-spawn ritual, and are not interested in food. Those massed closer to bottom, on the other hand, are likely to take, so the skippers pay a lot more attention to the tarpon they see on their depthfinders than those they see on top.

In general, the feeding fish are most often found on the ledge of the up-current side of the deeper holes, so the top skippers spend a lot of time working over these locations, pinpointing them by lining up the Lighthouse and the fuel storage tanks ashore as markers for the various hotspots.

When a tarpon takes, there's no mistaking it. The heavy rod takes on an alarming bend, and as soon as it does the skipper firewalls the throttle. This takes up slack, drives the hook home, and gets the boat out of the way in case the fish decides to come straight up and jump, as they often do. (A green tarpon inside a boat's cockpit is an awesome sight. The only thing to do is take cover, anywhere you can find it, until the fish jumps back out or expires.)

"The one problem a lot of beginners have is that they want to jerk on the rod to set the hook," notes Jon Zorian. "It doesn't work most of the time. You can't jerk hard enough to get all the slack out and drive the barb home, but you can jerk

Capt. Jon Zorian goes over the fine points of setting the hook when tarpon fishing in Boca Grande pass.

hard enough to make him spit out the bait. I make all my customers keep their hands on top of the rod, not under it, so they can't reflexively set the hook when they get a strike."

Zorian also adds a length of split plastic hose to the lower section of his rods, where they cross the gunnel, as a cushion and to prevent the rod from slipping at the strike.

Jigging The Pass

For years most anglers believed that only live bait would catch Boca Grande tarpon, but about 20 years ago some innovative anglers, including Vic Dunaway of Florida Sportsman Magazine and Herb Allen of the Tampa Tribune began experimenting with medium-weight jigs, and soon discovered that the tarpon took them very well with the right presentation.

These days, a few guides like Charlie Cleveland of Tampa specialize in jigging the pass, and even the old hard-line Boca Granders are starting to switch over, because the jigs work better than live baits on occasion.

Most use jigs weighing from 1 to 4 ounces, built on long-shank 5/0 to 7/0 hooks. Large plastic "swimmer tails" from Cotee, Bubba or 12-Fathom are added to provide color and action. The whole lure is about 5 inches long, not large considering the size of a tarpon.

Two feet of 80-pound-test mono is used as shock leader against the rough jaws of the fish.

81

Using either medium saltwater spinning gear with 25-pound-test or revolving spool reels with 30 to 40-pound test, the jigs are tossed down-current as far as possible in an area where the depthfinder shows lots of fish. The jig is allowed to sink as the angler takes in slack, with the boat drifting toward the spot where the jig hit the water. As soon as the jig touches bottom, it's jigged upward in a series of short twitches. You get perhaps 15 to 20 seconds of "bottom time" for each cast, not much, but often it's enough. As soon as the jig stops making bottom contact, it's reeled up and cast ahead of the drift once again.

Anglers are also discovering that drifting sinking plugs through the pass can be effective. Using a technique developed in the Caribbean off Costa Rica, anglers suspend a heavy sinking plug like a 65 or 72-M MirrOlure straight down, just off bottom, and let the drift of the boat and the wave action make it appear alive. It's a new method, little known at this writing, but those who have tried it are reporting good success.

Fishing The Hill
Sometimes the fish move out of the depths of the pass and go on a feeding binge "on the hill" or in the shallower approaches to the holes. These feeds are usually announced by crashing explosions as the fish slam into crabs or baitfish working along the surface.

When the surface activity is noted, many experts remove all the weight from their baits and free-line or "fly-line" them behind the drifting boat, juggling the throttle to allow a natural drift. When things are right, hooking four or more fish per tide is a possibility with this technique.

Pass Etiquette
The Boca Grande Fishing Guide's Association leaflet "Tarpon Fishing and Boat Operation at Boca Grande Pass" is a remarkably unselfish gift from the guides association at Boca Grande. The flyer, in a single reading, can turn a rank amateur into a passable tarpon fisherman. It holds little back, revealing most of the secrets of successfully connecting with tarpon in the deep, swift waters of the pass.

Well, maybe it's not totally unselfish. Actually, the guides released the leaflet when they realized that boat traffic was

Typical pass tarpon weigh 60 to 90 pounds. They're often seen rolling in schools of a hundred or more, but rolling fish rarely bite. The ones that are caught are the thousands that hold close to bottom in the 72-foot depths.

becoming totally unmanageable in the pass, and that a set of "traffic rules" known to everyone was needed. Thus, the leaflet is long on boat-handling advice, as well as on the how-to of fish catching.

There are days when more than a hundred boats jam into the pass, drifting close enough to bump rubrails.

Nobody ever shuts off his engine in the pass, because to do so invites disaster as a big cruiser bears down on you--and you also may need a quick burst of power to tighten the line and set the hook on a silver king.

Basically, the leaflet tells how to set up to drift with the wind and tide over the length of the hole, maintaining your distance and traveling along with all the other boats in the fleet--you manage this by keeping the engine running and bumping it in and out of gear to maintain steerage and keep your lines going straight down instead of ballooning out behind the boat. One angler must devote all his time to handling the boat, watching the depthfinder, and keeping an eye on the traffic.

When a drift is completed, it's essential for boats at the lower end of the drift to pick up their lines and motor in a wide, low-speed arc outside the drifting fleet, rather than running right back up through them. A boat going the wrong direction has the same effect as a wrong-way drunk on an interstate highway, and draws the same sort of angry reactions.

It's also not kosher to anchor in the pass. A single anchored boat becomes an obstacle for every other boat in the fleet. And you're unlikely to get your anchor back, in any case, because of the snagging rocks on the bottom. In fact, anchoring a small boat can be dangerous due to the strong tide flows, up to six knots, and the frequently rough seas in the inlet.

It's also necessary to get out of the way of any boat chasing a hooked fish. If you cut their line with your prop, you'll be on the receiving end of some of the remarkably creative invective of the Boca Grande boatmen.

You can get your brochure by sending a stamped, self-addressed envelope to Boca Grande Fishing Guides Association, P.O. Box 676, Boca Grande, FL 33921. The leaflet also contains the names and phone numbers of all charterboat captains.

Accommodations

Boca Grande is an expensive place to stay, with the most basic accommodations starting at $100 per night, and a hamburger going for $5 in most restaurants. (An exception is the upstairs dining room at Miller's Marina, where the food is inexpensive and good, and the tin-roof, open air ambiance to most angler's liking.)

Launching ramps are scarce, and you must pay up to $10 per use to put in--this on top of the fee to cross the toll bridge to get on the island. It's unfortunate, but the residents understandably don't want to be over-run by "off-islanders." If you can afford it, the South Pacific ambiance of the island and the town is delightful, one of the world's fine getaways.

While you're in the neighborhood, you might want to stop in at Cabbage Key, where there's a truly unique island restaurant hidden among the mangroves. The place is close to a century old, and some say it's held together by the thousands of yellowed dollar bills left stuck to the ceiling by guests. It's getting a bit crowded these days due to tour boats, and there's usually a line at lunch and dinner, but if you go at off hours you can enjoy the good but pricey food in a place where you just know Jimmy Buffet would love to waste away.

CHAPTER 11

CHARLOTTE HARBOR AND TAMPA BAY

NINETY SEVEN DEGREES. That's what the thermometer on the boat shed said when we left the ramp at El Jobean, the tiny river-crossing town on the Myakka River, where the coffee black water flows into the northern tip of Charlotte Harbor. It was one of those windless, breathless August afternoons, when the only things that stir are the no-see-ums, chomping tiny openings in your neck where the salty sweat stings. T-shirts plastered to our backs, and the decks of Bill Miller's flats boat were hot enough to melt the rubber on the bottom of my deck shoes.

We were neither mad dogs nor Englishmen, but tarpon addicts, in search of a late summer fix. And before long, we got it. Within 30 minutes of the docks, we stopped in what must have been the mother lode. Where ever we looked on the mirrored, black surface, there were reddish fins of tarpon poking through the surface, or the silvered backs porpoising out, or the shovel-wide tails slapping at the water.

I tossed a 65-MirrOlure, a slow-sinking mullet imitation, toward the nearest fish, let it sink--and came up with nothing.

"You have to allow for the water depth," Bill told me. "Cast it far enough ahead of them so that it's down near the bottom by the time they get there. They roll, and then they go right back down to look for food."

Since the water was close to 20 feet deep in the area we were fishing, that was a considerable allowance. I tried to

The usually calm waters of the Harbor in summer makes it possible to fish the tarpon in small rigs, including bass boats. Baitcasting rigs and slow-sinking plugs are favored.

figure the trajectory of the next fish that rolled within range, casting so that the lure landed at least 30 feet in front of him.

I waited a long 15 seconds as the 17-pound-test mono followed the lure into the depths. Suddenly, I saw the line jump forward, a brief tick. When I reared back on the stout, two-handed baitcaster, six feet of twisting, shaking silver, exploded the calm of the quiet afternoon. The fish came up in three more majestic, slow-motion leaps, each time farther away. When it was about a hundred yards out, the final leap sent the plug sailing 20 feet in the air.

Remarkably, when I had retrieved the lure to within about 50 feet of the boat, another fish grabbed it. I was so amazed I didn't set the hook, so it spit the plug with a single, contemptuous roll of the head. But after that, I treated every cast with considerable respect.

In the next two hours, we jumped five more fish, including a hundred-pounder that Bill whipped in about 30 minutes of heavy work, the sweat pouring off him. We photographed the fish, then revived it and allowed it to swim off.

Charlotte Harbor Tarpon

Miller should get enough of the silver kings earlier in the year, since he's usually booked solid from May through July as one of the better-known tarpon guides at Florida's famed Boca Grande Pass, on the west coast about 100 miles south of

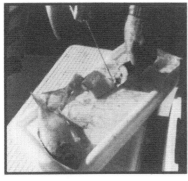
Cut menhaden makes an excellent chum for backwater tarpon. A whole menhaden is used as bait.

Tampa. But the guiding action comes to an abrupt halt when the semi-official season ends July 31. The fish disappear then--perhaps traveling offshore to spawn--and all the visiting anglers go home.

Miller wondered where the fish went after the spawn. In early summer, there are literally thousands of adult tarpon in the pass, often rolling at the surface in massive, splashing schools of 100 or more at a time. But all those fish pull up stakes and vanish in August, not to be seen again until the following spring.

He had some hints from older guides on these waters, who occasionally caught fish in the eastern section of Charlotte Harbor, the 25-mile long dog-legged bay that feeds the pass, by trolling big spoons through open water in late summer. Others made good catches by drowning cut shad on bottom, putting out a spread of four to eight rods after chumming the area with a dozen or more cut-up baits.

If there were enough tarpon around to find the spoons and the cut bait fished randomly through the open water, Miller and a few other anglers surmised, there might be a mother-lode in there somewhere, perhaps the major concentration of fish from the pass, or at least a part of that giant aggregation--maybe enough fish for some serious light tackle action.

Where To Hunt

The day we visited, our first stop was in the neck of open water just south of El Jobean, above the area where the Peace River enters at Port Charlotte to make up the main body of the harbor. The technique of finding fish was much like that used in the Florida Keys or at Homosassa, drifting silently, both of us alert for the slightest ripple, splash, or silver flash that might indicate tarpon at the surface. The difference here was that we were looking for fish in water 8 to 20 feet deep, and because of the deep tannin stain, there was no possibility of seeing fish cruising past underwater. The MirrOlures we had tied to our two-hand baitcasters disappeared less than two feet under the surface, even when dropped right at boatside.

Miller and others like Captain Paul Hawkins who have become successful at finding fish in the upper harbor say that it's a matter of moving until you come on an area where there are considerable numbers of tarpon showing, rather than stopping at random for blind casts. In any reasonably calm weather, it's not difficult to see the fish on top. Sometimes they only reveal themselves by the slightest dimple of the water as the tip of a tail or a fin pokes through. At other times, they explode, greyhounding completely out of the water, almost like free-jumping sailfish, as they chase bait--or sometimes, simply play with their schoolmates.

Though we found good action in the afternoon, Miller says finding fish is usually easiest in the morning, because the water is more often calm then. By 9 a.m., it's not uncommon for a breeze to spring up off the nearby Gulf, and frequently in August, afternoon brings violent thunderstorms. Best action is from first light until an hour or two after sunrise most days.

The action generally ends in October, with most of the fish heading offshore. However, a fair contingent probably wind up in the Caloosahatchee River, south of the Harbor, at the outflow of the Orange River. A powerplant discharge feeds in here, and the water stays warm all winter, providing a refuge for the tarpon. Best action is east of the I-75 bridge, best bait a slow-trolled live mullet.

Tampa Bay Tarpon

Tampa Bay, about 100 miles north of Charlotte Harbor, has similar fishing despite being much more developed and with poorer water quality.

According to Capt. Paul Hawkins, who specializes in this area, tarpon show up first at Bean Point, off the north tip of

Guide Bill Miller tangles with a backwater tarpon in Charlotte Harbor during late summer. Hundreds of fish move up from Boca Grande Pass to the tannin-stained waters of the harbor from August through early October.

Anna Maria Island, and at Passage Key, in May. Both areas have clear water and sparkling white sand bottom, making them ideal for fly fishing.

However, both areas are small and extremely sensitive to angling pressure. Neither flat can handle more than three boats, so unless you get there first, it's best to let the early risers have it and come back another day. Crowding in on other boats only results in nobody catching fish.

The technique at these spots is to stake out and wait for fish to pass across the flats, hopefully within range. If the wind blows hard out of the south or west, the location is unfishable, but when it's calm and the fish are in, it can be a real hotspot.

The Sunshine Skyway Pier, the world's longest fishing pier, is also an excellent tarpon spot. All the bait that goes in and out of Tampa Bay passes through this span, so it's a natural for tarpon. Many fish are hooked right off the bridge each summer, and occasionally some very large ones, to 170 pounds, are landed.

This is naturally heavy-tackle action, with 50-pound-class tackle and up needed to have any hope of holding the fish away from the pilings. Live mullet, menhaden and crabs are good baits hung out under a float, or sometimes anchored to bottom near the edge of the main channel.

Capt. Charlie Cleveland does well on tarpon at both Charlotte Harbor and Tampa Bay by fishing jigs in the deep passes.

Tarpon move up inside the bay in late summer, with good fishing usually starting in July. They're found in the deep, open sections of the bay, average depth of about 20 feet, in areas such as the "Middle Grounds" off St. Petersburg's downtown pier. Fish are also spotted at times outside the MacDill flats, and off the long bar at Apollo Beach.

The technique is to pray for calm, then motor the bay slowly as the sun rises, looking for rolling fish. When a location is found with a number of fish, the boat is anchored and the chumming begins.

Menhaden, lightly salted and aged on ice a day or two to toughen it, is the ticket for chum, and also as bait. It's fished on bottom, on 40-pound tackle. You catch a lot more sailcats than tarpon, but in a good year this is a dependable way to jump a fish or two daily.

Tarpon also gather in Old Tampa Bay, between Gandy and Howard Frankland bridges, in late summer. Fishing around the bridge spans is particularly good after dark, when tarpon, snook and other species school to feed on baitfish attracted by the bridge lights. A jumbo shrimp is a hard bait to beat if there are lots of tarpon and not too many ladyfish. Otherwise, offer finger mullet, pinfish, or sinking plugs.

90

This whopper tarpon was taken from Tampa Bay by Donna Salmon during the annual Hillsborough Tarpon Tournament. Tarpon gather in the bay in good numbers in late summer and early fall.

Baby tarpon to 15 pounds are frequently found up the Little Manatee River at Ruskin in summer, and at the Big Bend and Gandy powerplant outflows in winter. They take small, gold-finish jigs in all three spots.

Tackle For Bay Tarpon

Best tackle for catching bay tarpon is probably the gear we used at Charlotte Harbor, seven-foot rods with very stout bases, tapering to a light tip capable of casting the light plugs long distances.

Medium-sized baitcasting reels like the Ambassadeur 6000, loaded with 15 to 20 pound test line, are up to the task of handling even the occasional big fish, over 100 pounds. The line is doubled with a Bimini twist, to which about 10 feet of 30-pound leader is added to prevent abrasion from the rough scales of the tarpon in a long struggle. A foot of 80 to 100-pound mono is added as shock leader to prevent abrasion by the rough jaws.

All connections are made with blood knots, Uni-knots or other line-to-line connections, rather than swivels, so that the connections go through the guides smoothly on casting.

91

The lure is tied on with a loop knot, so that the plug swings free on the stout shock leader.

For baitfishing, most anglers like heavier gear, 4/0 reels and matching rods loaded with 40-pound or better. An egg sinker large enough to hold bottom against the current is added.

A major part of success in plug casting is a boat that can be moved into range of the fish silently. Since the water is generally too deep for a push pole, an electric trolling motor is a necessity. The fish are fairly tolerant of the whir of the electrics in the deep, dark water, but best action results when the motor is turned on just long enough to get the boat into position near a school. The boat is then allowed to drift as the fish pass within casting range.

Fishing this way often puts the boat near enough to the fish for a flyrod presentation, and tarpon are noted for their affinity for a streamer of moderate size. In clear water, they'll take the fly quicker than any larger artificial, and often quicker than a juicy live bait.

In the dingy water of Charlotte Harbor and Tampa Bay, they also take flies occasionally, but the offering has to be right on the money, passing within a couple of feet of the nose of the fish, or it won't be seen. This makes fly-rodding a challenge, but still a possibility for those skilled with the long rod. Sinking tip lines are needed to bring the fly down to the level where the fish hit.

Fishing remains good throughout the hot weather of late summer, which extends at least until the end of September in Florida. The fish sometimes move further up the bays as the summer progresses, winding up well inside the rivers at times. Other years, if there are heavy rains in late summer, the freshet may push them far down the bay. Anglers who do a lot of running and looking consistently get on the main schools and have good action.

When the days start to shorten around mid-October and the frontal winds begin to blow, the fish move out, apparently migrating south until the cycle renews itself with the return to the big bays in May.

CHAPTER 12

TARPON ON THE BEACH

IT MAY BE Florida's best tarpon fishing, and it's almost unknown.

The west coast beaches from Tampa Bay to Marco Island hold an incredible concentration of fish from early May to mid-July. Yet on most weekday mornings, it's rare to spot another boat as you cast your plug or live bait at seemingly unlimited schools of passing fish.

A trip I made with Captain Kenny Shannon out of Venice Inlet, 60 miles south of Tampa, was typical. We left a public ramp just inside the inlet at first light, motored a few miles up the beach and spotted our first school as the sun began to rise.

"They're at 2 o'clock, a pod of 80-pounders," Shannon advised as he hit the switch on his twin 24-volt OMC trolling motors. The Mako 17 scooted to intersect the path of travel of the rapidly-moving fish, their broad, silver-green backs glinting in the early light. We were no more than 200 yards off the white sand of the beach.

When we were 30 yards away, both of us fired live blue crabs in their direction, throwing ahead of and beyond the school.

Buck fever time as the horse-like fish rolled toward the baits, gulping air through bucket-sized mouths.

My crab sank out of sight in the green water. I took up the bow of slack on the big spinning reel, scooting him directly into their path.

The line bounced, then straightened. I let the fish draw the rod tip down, then slapped the big 7/0 home with four quick jabs of the stout, 7-foot rod.

He instantly started doing those crazy tarpon things. The 5-foot missile launched straight into the rising sun, exploded back into the Gulf, swapped ends, grayhounded twice, did a tail-standing head shake that rattled his gills, and then tore off 150 yards of line as the drag on the big Penn howled.

"We're having fun now," Shannon grinned, easing after the fish on the trolling motor.

Twenty minutes later the fish yielded to the insistent pressure of the 25-pound-test mono and gasped at boatside. Shannon used a lip-gaff to hold him for pictures and tagging, then eased him back to swim away.

Shannon didn't bother to start the engine.

"There's another pod coming right at us," he said, pointing out the distant fish.

Ten minutes later, we were fast to another tarpon.

And so it went throughout that long June morning. There was rarely 15 minutes when we were not within sight of fish or hooked up.

Shannon said his best days have produced as high as 19 hook-ups from dawn until noon. The average catch for the few guides who concentrate on the run is two fish brought to the boat daily, six to eight hooked.

Patterning Beach Tarpon

It's remarkable fishing, and yet only a few locals regularly enjoy it. It's ironic, considering that Boca Grande Pass, the world's best-known and hardest-fished tarpon spot, sits smack in the middle of this stretch of beach. While boats literally bump rubrails to get at the fish in the big pass, the thousands of silver kings that roam the beaches are largely ignored.

Fishing can be good just about anywhere along the west coast beaches as far north as Clearwater in this period, but the fish show more consistently from Tampa Bay southward. The Venice to Boca Grande area is prime, as is the southern tip of Sanibel Island and the Fort Myers Beach area. Naples to Bonita Springs is also very strong.

According to Scott Moore, another premiere beach tarpon guide, the fish are found in water from 10 to 25 feet deep,

Capt. Kenny Shannon prepares to release a 90-pounder caught on a live crab off the beaches near Venice, FL. From May through July, hundreds of fish travel within a mile of southwest Florida beaches.

usually from 200 to 500 yards off the beach--they're thus accessible to boats of all sizes. They tend to travel parallel to the beach, moving steadily except for occasional stops to feed or "daisy chain". The school you want, Moore says, is the one that's lazing along and showing a lot--"happy 'poons" the guides call them--because they're much more likely to bite than fish that are moving along fast and rolling infrequently.

Shannon and other guides like Capt. Ad Gilbert use live blue crabs because the baits are durable, easy to cast and much-loved by the tarpon, but mullet, pinfish, sardines and other small baits are equally acceptable. The fish also readily take sinking plugs such as the Bagley Finger Mullet and the 65M-MirrOlure, and can also be caught on flies, though deep water makes it tough to get the streamer down to their level.

The fishing is so dependable that Shannon once went 47 days in a row without a wash, tagging at least one fish daily and sometimes up to 10.

The fish are big, but not the giants found further north at the Homosassa flats. Most run between 50 and 80 pounds, though occasionally a monster female in the 150-pound-class crashes the show.

Most anglers use medium spinning tackle with 20- to 25-pound test mono. Those with educated thumbs use large revolving spool reels on 8-foot rods, with 30-pound-test line. Some anglers prefer Dacron to mono, because there's less stretch on the hook set, and also because it floats, making it easy to see where the bait is. This tackle allows tarpon to strut their stuff, but when handled right has the authority to bring the average fish to the boat in under 20 minutes. This is good both for the angler and the fish, and makes it more certain that the tarpon will swim off to fight another day.

For fly-rodding, the usual 12-weight tackle with "slime-line" or the new Orvis "Tarpon Taper" with a clear, sinking tip is the ticket. (Ad Gilbert prefers floating, sink-tip lines because they allow a quicker lift off the water for a follow-up cast. He says a 10-foot sinking tip gets the fly down to the feeding level for most beach fish.) Pale green streamers do well in the generally clear water.

The action is best in the morning, when the sea is usually calm at this time of year. Shortly after noon, a westerly sea breeze springs up, making the water bumpy and also making it harder to see approaching fish.

The trick to getting bit consistently is to spot the fish at long range, run the boat around them in a broad circle that keeps you at least 300 yards away, and then shut down the outboard and let them swim into range as you make final adjustments with an electric trolling motor. (Sometimes, the fish don't roll as they approach--but may release a tell-tale string of bubbles as they exhale.)

The reason most amateurs have problems with beach fish is that they attempt to motor directly into casting range, which inevitably puts the fish down.

Presenting The Bait

Presentation is also a bit tricky. If you throw a slow-sinking bait directly in front of rolling fish, chances are that they'll pass under it without ever noticing. The successful cast lands about 50 feet ahead of the school, and has sunk down 6 to 10 feet by the time they arrive. There are usually lots of fish

Biologists have learned that tarpon can live for up to half a century, but are very slow-growing. Catch-and-release fishing is essential, many say, if mature fish are to be available in the future.

below and behind the leaders you see rolling on top, and these hidden fish are the ones that take most of the time.

Most guides use about 5 feet of 100-pound-test leader, tied to just enough double line to allow making a good line-leader connection. This rigging creates minimal casting problems, and gives the gaff man a "handle" to draw the tarpon in close for de-hooking. (Anglers who fish from boats with towers--which allow easier spotting of approaching fish--use longer leaders, up to 9 feet, and make the cast from the tower in a 360-degree "Cracker cast" that keeps everything straight and reaches tremendous distances.)

Shannon and some other guides are now using a unique hook produced by the Owner Corporation, known as the "Gorilla Big Game" version. It's aptly named, a forged monster of a hook that's about twice as thick as a normal saltwater hook, but has a razor edged shovel-point. The hook looks a bit like the circle hooks used by long-line fishermen, and has an uncanny ability to stay put in a tarpon's hard mouth. Prompt hook sets prevent gut hooking almost 100 percent of the time.

Hooking Beach Tarpon

Tarpon are among the toughest of all fish to hook, no doubt about it. But with the right techniques, you can win the game most of the time.

97

First, of course, the hooks must be razor-sharp, the line must be strong enough to stretch little at the set, and the rod must have all the whip of a shovel handle.

But just as importantly, according to Kenny Shannon, is letting the fish help you set the hook.

"If you throw to fish coming straight at you, you're going to have a very tough time setting the hook, because they keep right on moving as they eat the bait," he notes. "When you set, you've got instant slack, and you're pulling straight away from the fish--your chance of landing that fish is about zero."

Much better, he notes, is to make the presentation from the side, or in the case of live baits, even from slightly behind. You cast ahead of the fish and let them take going away.

"In this situation, the fish is taking the slack out of your line for you, and the set will pull the hook into the upper corner of his jaw, 95 percent of the time," he says.

Ad Gilbert agrees, and notes that most of the time it's not even necessary to set the hook, since the fish running against the drag will do the job for you.

Post-Spawn Patterns

The beach action stays good until about July 15 most years, at which time the fish pack up and head offshore, apparently to spawn at the edge of the continental shelf.

They don't all go at once, and the main body is back within a week, but the fishing changes a bit on the return. The schools are replaced by scattered, lone fish that don't travel in the same, one-directional pattern.

Shannon and other guides find fish then by drifting baits around schools of sardines, positioning the baits by looking for diving birds or splashing Spanish mackerel. The tackle is much the same, but it's blind fishing, with the bait suspended five feet below a cork. Not quite the same thrill as casting to moving fish, but it can be just as productive.

This action ends around the end of August, when most of the beach fish disappear. Whether they are among the same fish which stay late inside the larger bays or whether they travel south, or far offshore for the winter, remains to be seen, but it's sure they'll return in spring to provide the same great action for the few anglers in the know about beach fishing.

CHAPTER 13

ATLANTIC TARPON

THE ATLANTIC COAST is generally not so widely recognized as tarpon country as is the Gulf, but there can be remarkable numbers of fish off the beaches from Florida all the way to Cape Hatteras, North Carolina, in summer.

North Carolina

The Outer Banks of North Carolina create a remarkable confluence of gamefish thanks to their broad shoals, extending miles into the sea and generating enormous schooling areas for baitfish of many species. Tarpon are abundant in the area in summer.

Most famous spot is notorious Diamond Shoals at Cape Hatteras, the graveyard of the Atlantic for shipping, where a vast bar up to five miles wide extends more than 10 miles into the sea. Depth ranges from 20 to 50 feet on the shoal, dropping to a hundred beyond the tip. The eddies and upwellings generated by the shoal hold baitfish for months at a time, and create a great feeding ground for all sorts of gamefish including tarpon.

Hatteras Bight and Hatteras Inlet, to the south of the shoals, also hold fish in summer and as late as October most years.

The deep hole in close to the beach on Bogue Banks, near Swansboro, is a noted spot for tarpon and jumbo king mackerel.

Tarpon are also occasionally spotted working the menhaden schools around the piers at Morehead City--and some tarpon are caught right from the piers, though chances of landing a fish are a lot better from a boat. And the outer edge of Cape Lookout Shoals, an extreme shoal with breakers common most of the time, also holds fish in summer. Further south, Frying Pan Shoals extending off Cape Fear has good tarpon action from June through October in the finger channels of deeper water that cut through shoal areas of 15-20 feet.

Throughout North Carolina waters, menhaden is hard to beat, both as a chum and as a live or dead bait. It's readily cast-netted along the beaches with a large diameter net with heavy leads, and can be kept lively in a large flow-through live well.

Most anglers fish the baits nose-hooked on 4/0 short shank hooks, suspending them under a float around the shoals or in areas where tarpon are seen rolling, or sometimes anchoring them to bottom in the deeper sloughs.

Shrimp Boat Action

In June, July and August, considerable numbers of tarpon gather behind the shrimp boats anchored off the beaches from St. Augustine northward, and put to use what this wasteful method of fishing discards. The fish are not monsters, with most running 80 to 100 pounds, but they're plenty big enough when they start to cavort against the sky. And, when the chum is heavy, it's not uncommon to connect with 8 or 10 fish in a morning, though many part company promptly.

Many anglers catch tarpon along this section of coast with live menhaden, netted from schools found along the beach and around the markers. Live sugar trout and ladyfish are also popular baits. The baits may be put out to drift with the chum, or anchored on bottom with a couple ounces of lead. If the lead is used, it's generally wired to the swivel with light copper wire, so that it gets tossed clear on the first leap, ala Boca Grande rigging.

When the shrimpers are not around, you can create your own chum line by cutting up menhaden. Smaller menhaden can be caused to float by injecting air into their stomachs with a hypodermic needle, available from veterinarians.

100

Finding just the right spot off the Atlantic Coast sometimes takes a bit of help such as that provided by this hand-held LORAN. Tarpon abound along the Atlantic shores so long as water temperature remains above 72 degrees.

Many anglers still make use of chum bought from the shrimpers, but more and more refuse to deal with them because of the tremendous waste of juvenile fish--10 pounds of "by-catch" for every pound of shrimp caught. Follow your own conscience.

Because of the relatively deep water--20 to 60 feet--tackle for this sort of fishing is usually conventional revolving spool reels and 40- to 50-pound test. It can be hard to get a tarpon up with lighter gear, though those with plenty of skill and will power can manage it--if the sharks don't take an interest in their tiring fish.

The fishing in this area remains good until the first chilly, northeast blow of late fall, when they vanish overnight, moving either offshore to the edge of the Gulf Stream or south to warmer climes.

South Florida

There are fewer shrimpers, but as many tarpon, as you move south along Florida's Atlantic shore. The big shoals at Cape Canaveral is a good area all summer long. So are the inlets further south, including Sebastian, Fort Pierce, St. Lucie and Jupiter. In general, you find the fish where you find bait, which may be right against the beach, or several miles out.

101

There are also good schools of smaller tarpon inside the rivers at times, with large numbers in the Sebastian and St. Lucy in late summer.

Anglers fish for mature tarpon along the beaches where they see them, and in calm weather it's possible to connect both by drifting live baits and by pitching sinking plugs. The big teak versions from Trader Bay, made in the Canaveral area, are popular.

Tarpon are particularly partial to threadfin herring or greenbacks, and these abundant baitfish are often found schooled over small "patch"reefs in 10 to 30 feet of water, usually within a couple hundred yards of the surf. Anglers net their baits out of the schools and put them right back out in the same area to connect.

The Mullet Run

Fishing is good all summer, great during the mullet run, northward in spring, southward in fall. Spring action is in April and May, ending by early June. The fall action is most predictable, and most remarkable. Prime time begins in mid-September and extends through October, peaking in each area as the mullet run peaks. The fishing is usually best from Canaveral southward, getting good in South Florida in late September after the first fronts arrive to run the fish off from more northern beaches.

It's almost too easy at times. The mullet gather in thousands, a seemingly endless line stretching along the slough and sometimes right up into knee-deep water, and the fish--both tarpon and many monster snook--follow along.

Experts like Capt. Mike Holliday of Stuart wear the fish out right off the beach. The routine is to carry a castnet and a five gallon bucket, net up three or four mullet 6-8 inches long, stow them in the bucket, and run one out unweighted on a 3/0 to 5/0 hook.

Lip-hooking is good for durability, but some anglers prefer to place the hook behind the dorsal, so that they can hold a bit of back-pressure on the mullet and cause it to flip and flutter at the surface--the tarpon can't stand it.

The bait is fished right in the midst of the rest of the school, but when a fish approaches, you'll notice that the schoolmates disappear as if a wind has blown them off. When

102

Shrimp boats provide a chum line for both birds and tarpon when they sort their catch. Many anglers take advantage of the chum line created--though others protest the waste resulting from destruction of juvenile fish by the shrimp nets.

your bait is suddenly swimming alone, hang on and get set for the explosion.

Revolving spool reels that will hold 350 yards of 30 are needed to give you much of a chance at landing the tarpon, because many head for the Bahamas when hooked. Even at that, expect to do a lot of running up and down the beach, following the run of a hooked fish as you try to keep a few turns of line on the spool. Some anglers use the largest of surf-type saltwater spinning reels and 30 pound test with good results. The spinner makes casting easier for most fishermen.

Often, a cast of only 20 feet will put you in the fish, as the tarpon push the bait right up against the sand. Pros walk the beach, or drive in 4WD's in the more northern sections where beach traffic is legal, looking for areas where the mullet are "showering" or jumping into the air. This indicates big fish working on the bait--a good place to offer them a live one--or the new, remarkably life-like DOA finger mullet, a soft plastic that imitates the natural almost perfectly.

Areas within a quarter-mile either side of any inlet are usually particularly productive, as the baitfish work in and out of the backwaters with the tide flows.

So long as winds remain moderate and the surf is clear, the fishing holds up. This can run into November some years.

Other years, the first big northern fronts arrive in late October--and some years a late tropical storm mucks up the water and blows the fish out early.

In winter, tarpon become harder to find, but some pod up on the inside in deep areas with warm water flow, such as around the power plant at Port Everglades.

There's also outstanding deep water fishing in Government Cut at Miami throughout the winter, with both live baits on bottom and jigs and sinking plugs effective. The deep water in this dredged channel provides insulation for the fish, and the enclosed area is fishable even when cold fronts blow through. Capt. Bouncer Smith and others are past masters at this fishing, producing near perfect success rates when the fish are "on". There's probably no better tarpon hole on the east coast.

CHAPTER 14

TARPON OF TEXAS, LOUISIANA AND THE NORTHERN GULF

LIKE WEALTHY TOURISTS, the silver king likes to take stylish northern vacations in summer. Tarpon are seasonally abundant in the northern Gulf of Mexico, from the Florida Panhandle and the Mississippi Delta all the way around the beach to Brownsville, Texas.

The Florida Panhandle

In the panhandle, the tarpon generally come late, with action getting good in July and continuing through early October.

Tarpon fishing is not well developed here, but there are good numbers of fish in many areas.

Some of the noted locations are Ochlockonee Bay and Alligator Point east of Carrabelle, Mud Cove, Turkey Point and the mouth of Carrabelle River, and sometimes East Pass, between Dog Island and St. George Island.

The deep grass flats inside St. George also hold fish at times, and this is one of the few areas in North Florida where sight-casting with fly tackle is practical due to the clear water. The water gets murky on the inside, but the fish are there more dependably, around the shrimp docks at the mouth of Apalachicola River, and in East Bay, the big eastern arm of the Apalachicola Delta. West Pass, which separates St. George Island from St. Vincent Island, is good, as is Indian Pass, separating St. Vincent from Indian Peninsula. The latter is a protected pass fishable when strong winds make the other areas difficult.

Cape San Blas has fish at times, and in calm weather they take plugs close to the beach. Otherwise, it's pretty much bait fished on bottom.

Tarpon sometimes move into Choctawhatchee Bay, but not many locals pursue them. They can also be sighted rolling outside East Pass at Destin in late summer, but again, few resident anglers who concentrate on patterning the fish. The mouth of Alabama's Perdido River also occasionally produces some big fish in fall.

Louisiana Giants

Louisiana is becoming known as the place to go for giant tarpon. Though the murky waters at the mouth of the Mississippi do not look like classic tarpon waters at all, the rich feeding areas here attract and hold enormous schools of mature fish in late summer. It's possible that these waters are a gathering area after the bluewater spawns of early summer, perhaps an area for tarpon from many parts of the Gulf to restore their weight and strength before the southward migrations begin.

In any case, there are loads of big fish in bayou country.

One of the anglers who lands the lunkers most often is Captain Dave Ballay, who with his wife Debbie brings more than a hundred fish per season to his boat.

Ballay fishes out of the oil-rigging town of Venice, about an hour's drive south of New Orleans and maybe 30 minutes from the area where the Delta dumps its load of muddy water into the gulf. The mix of huge volumes of muddy fresh water with the clear but salty gulf creates a tremendously fertile area for bait production, and the tarpon take advantage of it.

The big push of fish shows up in August and stays through September, with most of the fishing in the larger bays of the Delta and close outside them, with depths ranging from 20 to 80 feet.

The classic techniques of drifting live or dead bait work well here, but in recent years Dave Ballay has been fishing

Silver kings show at Apalachicola Bay in mid-summer. Most are caught on natural bait fished on bottom, but plug-casters connect also.

something called a "Coon Pop tarpon jig", a big lead head with a twisting plastic tail, that makes the fish crazy. It uses a circle hook trailer that greatly increases the number of hooked fish. Ballay finds fish schools on sonar, motors over them, then cuts the throttle to let the baits plunge through the schools.

Ballay and others employ the same short, stout "stand-up" rods they use offshore for tuna, with impressive results. Using a fighting belt and the great leverage of these short rods, they bring 150-pound tarpon to the boat in minutes rather than hours. The result, says Ballay, is that the fish survive a lot better when released.

Venice and nearby Grand Isle, another noted spot for tarpon charters, are not exactly the garden spots of the South. They're working towns, and look it. But accommodations are good and fishermen are appreciated and catered to at both locations. You can also arrange combined trips to sample the incredible trout and redfishing, probably the world's best, in the bayou country--and if you want to run up the river instead of down, there's also great largemouth fishing here. To say nothing of crawfish. They eat spiced, boiled crawfish in this country like most folks eat potato chips. They serve them in gallon buckets. Lordy!

Texas Tarpon

In Texas, Captain Mike Williams of the Tarpon Express Guide Service in Galveston has quietly been making outstanding catches of tarpon for more than 30 years--but lately the secret has been leaking out.

"We've always had fine fishing here," says Williams. "It's just that nobody knew about it until five years ago."

Williams says the fish show up when the water temperature hits 70 degrees, usually in April. They stay in his fishing area--ranging from Sabine Pass to Port O'Conner--until early October, leaving when the water temperature drops out of the 70's.

Captain Joe Mauro of Houston is also a leading Texas tarpon guru. Mauro averages close to a fish per day during the prime August through October season, and notes that the fish run big--145 pounds was his average fish last season, with the biggest a hulking 188, the smallest a respectable 96-pounder.

"Tarpon fishing in Texas is all in the Gulf," says Mauro. "The fish rarely go inside unless we have several days of light, southwest winds that push in the bait but don't muddy the water."

He notes that the fish are caught from right in the surf line out to as much as 10 miles offshore, with the best action often found at 3-4 miles in water 20 to 32 feet deep.

"We fish underwater structure, sunken barges and the remains of old, stubbed-off oil wells, quite a bit," says Mauro. "And, when the shrimpers are sorting their catch, there are very often tarpon behind them picking up the by-catch."

He says that the tarpon congregate around any sort of structure because most of the bottom is flat mud, providing little habitat for bait. The stubbed off wells, even though they protrude only a couple of feet, often provide excellent action for those with the right LORAN numbers. Around the structure, most anglers dribble chum over the side to attract fish to their baits, but chum is not used behind the shrimpers since the by-catch provides a feast for both sharks and tarpon there.

Most fish are caught on natural baits, including ribbonfish, shad and mullet. The baits are fished dead, either drifting on

Beach tarpon also readily take a variety of jigs and sinking plugs. One of the secrets of success is casting well ahead of moving fish, so that the lure sinks to their level as they arrive.

a flatline or down deep off a downrigger ball, a technique Mauro is presently pioneering in Texas waters.

Captain Mike Williams also likes live baits, fishing live mullet when the tarpon are close to the beach, but switching to croaker or sand trout further out.

"The fish get right up against the shore when the water gets clear and they can see the mullet in there," says Williams, "but most of the time our catches come from 30 to 50 feet of water." Williams drifts the baits, unweighted, behind the boat.

He also reports an occasional run of very large fish inside Galveston Bay.

"It's not dependable, but the fish that go in the bay are always big ones. You never catch one under 150, and usually they're bigger than that."

Tackle is generally on the stout side, 30 to 50 pound gear. Mauro likes Newell reels and matching Fenwick rods about 6 1/2 to 7 feet long. He uses six feet of 125-pound-test mono as leader, and attaches a # 15 circle hook to hold the bait.

"Circle hooks look like they wouldn't catch anything, but we've found the hooking percentage is as high as 80 percent,

The tarpon along the beaches are not hard-fished, and usually are easy to hook. Getting them to the boat is another matter.

while with straight shank hooks we get 55 to 60 percent. They really work," says Joe.

Where do the tarpon go when they're not in Texas waters? Mike Williams thinks that two migrations mingle in the northern Gulf, with fish from Mexico and Central America pushing up along the western rim of the Gulf in spring and back in fall. And, he believes, a second group come from the Caribbean up through the Florida Keys, past Homosassa and into the area of the Mississippi Delta, finally spreading out as far as Galveston.

"The late fish are the big ones, and we've had a few tagged fish caught that were from Florida," says Williams.

When the western migration leaves the Galveston area in early to mid-October, they work south along the beaches, providing good fishing off Brownsville and Port Isabel into

110

November before heading south of the border. Large numbers seem to congregate there in the Port Isabel Channel before they push on south for the winter. In fact, the channel was the source of the current state record, a 210-pounder caught by Tom Gibson.

There are few brackish bayous along the Texas coast to encourage young tarpon to rear here, and the cold snaps of winter would probably be too much for these tropical fish in any case, so the fishery these days is pretty much confined to migrating fish in the open Gulf. But it's dependable and the fish run big--it's a growing and exciting fishery, at least in terms of the numbers of anglers learning how to connect.

On the down side, Texas' tarpon populations have shown what the Texas Parks and Wildlife Department calls a "statistically significant decline" in the last decade, and there's a concern that more anglers learning the ropes may hasten the drop in numbers. For that reason, in 1991, TP&W closed all harvest of tarpon, though catch-and-release remains open.

Many Texas tarpon anglers are calling for a small "window" to allow harvest of record fish, perhaps via paying a fee to the fisheries division, ala Florida's permit system.

Texas biologists, among the most innovative in the nation with regard to sport fishing, are also trying to spawn and rear tarpon in hatcheries.

With harvest controls in place and more anglers learning the tricks of taking the big tarpon of the northern Gulf, it could well be a hotspot for anglers in search of record fish in the 90's--though, if you catch that record in Texas under current regulations, you won't be able to land it!

CHAPTER 15

TROPICAL OPPORTUNITIES

THE HEART OF TARPON territory is not the southeastern United States, where the species is most heavily fished, but in the tropics themselves, throughout the Caribbean shore of Central and South America, and along the Atlantic Shore of East Africa. In the endless summers there, the fish reach their maximum abundance, and probably their maximum size as well.

Central America

Tarpon fishing is best-developed in Costa Rica, where a half-dozen camps cater to North American anglers.

The fish gather in the mouths of the jungle rivers, as well as in the surf and the adjacent deep water up to several miles offshore. At times, they can be incredibly abundant.

A trip I made out of Rio Colorado Lodge a few years ago was typical. We motored through the rather bumpy Rio Colorado Inlet, filled with the brown runoff of the uplands, to find the open sea beyond the same pale green as that in Florida. Water depth was about 30 to 50 feet, and fish were rolling everywhere.

The guide offered us red and white 65 M MirrOlures, which he assured us were sure-fire plugs. But when I cast one and began to work it with the usual series of twitches, he wagged a finger at me.

"No move," he advised in crippled English. "No move at all."

Still-fishing with artificial plugs was news to me, but I make it a practice to listen to the advice of guides wherever I go. I hung the lure straight down, just off bottom, as the boat drifted. We rocked gently in the low seas for about five minutes.

"I'll be surprised if this works," I told my angling partner, John Gillette of Tampa.

About that time, John's rod bent double and he was fast to a 120-pound tarpon.

When that fish was subdued about 40 minutes later, we hung the lures over the side again. Again, in less than five minutes, we had a strike, on my plug this time. The rod bounced, then doubled over as the fish inhaled the lure.

And so it went. It began to rain as it only rains in the tropics, a steady, straight-down deluge, without wind, seemingly without end, a rain so thick that we couldn't see from one end of the 20-foot boat to the other.

But the tarpon continued to bite, and we continued to fish. At one point, a hooked fish came rocketing out of the downpour to slam into the bow of the boat so hard it stove a plank--about three feet in front of my face.

There was never more than five minutes between strikes, and based on the number of fish, I suspect there never would have been, had we stayed out there all night. Absolutely incredible numbers of incredibly hungry fish.

In some of the more remote rivers, the fish also gather in great numbers on the inside, though that fishing has become less dependable in recent years as more camps have been built.

Word now is that there's great river fishing in Nicaragua, which is only a few miles up the coast from the mouth of the Rio Colorado. Those waters were untouched during the long Communist rule and the civil war, and now are providing great action in the more peaceful climate.

Fishing is good from January through early May, shuts down for the summer, and then is good again in September and October. An October bonus is the big snook that gather in the surf--the area produced the world all-tackle record.

The only problem with fishing the area is getting through the inlets. They can be exceedingly rough and dangerous, and

114

Tarpon are incredibly abundant in the Caribbean off the northeast shore of Costa Rica. On calm days, it's common to jump 15 to 20 fish. There are numerous modern fishing camps in the area.

some of the camps have only 16-foot jon boats to make the run. When it's rough, you don't fish--or you take a chance on running the inlet, which is a noted spot for shark attacks!

One camp has built a big "mother ship" to carry the jon boats out through the inlet in safety--but reportedly the jet drive system has not proven effective and it often sits at the dock. Rio Parismina Lodge is the first tarpon operation to bring in safe 21-1/2 foot center-console fiberglass boats.

Outside these difficulties, a visit to the Costa Rican coast is delightful. The camps are well-built and well-run, the food is good, and the locals remarkably friendly. The trip in includes an overnight in San Jose, a modern, pleasant, mountain city with lots of night life, plus a small plane flight through a mountain pass and over the jungle to the landing strips near the camps. It's a beautiful flight. Costa Rica is the most modern and most safe of Central American nations for U.S. citizens to visit.

Larger boats are slowly becoming available to allow getting safely through Costa Rican inlets. There's sometimes good fishing in the jungle rivers, as well.

Elsewhere In Central America

Belize also has a number of quality fishing lodges and houseboat operations, and some of them offer good tarpon fishing.

There's good action at the mouth of the Belize River pretty much year around, but action may be best in the winter months. Most fish are caught by casting topwaters and sinking plugs, but a few are hooked on flies as well. There's also good snook fishing in the same area.

Turneffe Island, which has a beautiful South Pacific- style lodge, also has pretty good tarpon fishing around its mangrove islands, with the action best in spring.

The water around this barrier island chain is very clear, so sight fishing is possible. It also offers great bonefish and permit water as a bonus, and you'll dine daily on fresh spiny lobster--and delicious barracuda filets, if you've got the nerve to eat them. Locals say there's never been a case of ciguetera from this stock of fish, and I ate a bunch of 'cuda during my last stay without ill effect.

116

Tarpon fishing is also good in the rivers and around the barrier islands of Belize. Quality camps and houseboats are available for traveling anglers.

The only bad thing about a visit to Belize is that you must pass through Belize City to get there. It is, truly, one of the armpits of the world, and North Americans are not well-liked there. Plan your trip so that you go direct to your camp on the day of arrival, with no stopover in the city, and you'll enjoy Belize. Ditto on the way back out--and be sure to confirm and reconfirm your flight reservations. Belize is among those third-world nations where advance airline reservations mean almost nothing.

Venezuela's Las Roques Islands, about 50 miles off the northern coast, have fair numbers of tarpon around the reefs that dot the clear channels between bonefish flats. The fishery is undeveloped at present, but could be a nice bonus for anglers who go there for the outstanding bonefishing. Accommodations are extremely limited, and there is neither air conditioning nor dependable running water on the islands. The flats fishing makes it worth while, anyway--and the mainland is a great place to visit, with outstanding restaurants, hotels and shopping.

117

There are also tarpon around the mouths of the jungle rivers that flow from the northeast shore of Venezuela and Brazil, but no fish camp has been established in the area as yet. The area could be a sleeper for future tarpon records. The all-tackle tarpon record, remember, came from Venezuela's Lake Maracaibo.

There are also monster tarpon--and no reasonable way to get at them--along the east coast of Africa, specifically in the area of Gabon. No less than six IGFA line-class records were set there in the 1980's, all six of them with fish over 200 pounds, and including the second-largest fish on record, a 248-pound, 3-ounce giant. Given the extremely low amount of recreational fishing that takes place in the area, the catches are truly phenomenal.

All the fish were landed out of the town of Port Michael, all in the deep, murky water at the mouth of the jungle river that enters the sea there. This is a primitive nation where things reportedly are not at all set up to the likings of North American anglers, but for the true adventurer with plenty of time, patience, money and chutzpah, a new all-tackle record may be waiting here.

For information on tour operators running trips to any of these nations, check the chapter on guides and camps.

CHAPTER 16

BOATS RIGGED FOR BATTLE

ASK THREE TARPON guides what makes the best boat for chasing silver kings and you'll likely get four opinions. This proves (a.) that tarpon guides are a cantankerous lot and (b.) that no boat is always perfect for all situations.

However, there are some basics that everybody will agree to most of the time, or at least before cocktail hour. (A lot of the original spadework for the modern flats boats was accomplished by Bob Hewes, the guru of shallow running from southern Florida. Hewes sold out to Maverick a few years back, but his mark is still seen both on the boats they produce under his name, and on many other brands.)

Boats For The Flats

Tarpon on the flats are frequently hard to find and often require all-day poling for the guy on the tower. Judging from back there after a 12-hour day, every angler wants a lighter boat.

And the current technology is turning out some very light ones, indeed. Using foam-core construction, a number of builders are producing 16- to 18-foot hulls that scale just over 700 pounds. These little jewels don't have a stick of wood in them, and they seem to sit on the water like a dry leaf, barely dimpling the surface.

Good tarpon boats for the flats are small, light, and loaded with storage space. Note the uncluttered look of the interior in this Silver King. Cleats and running lights are hidden away to prevent snagging flyline.

The 1,000-pound flats skiff of days gone by is now deemed too heavy by some, and most who chase tarpon for a living won't accept a hull that scales much over 850.

Going hand in hand with light weight is shallow draft. Tarpon boats don't have to float as high as bonefish boats because mature tarpon are just too big too venture into water much less than three feet deep. But, in order to get to some of those secret spots, you may have to jump a flat that's only 8 inches deep. Thus, boats that float and run very shallow are much coveted among silver king aficianados. At-rest drafts of as little as 7 inches are claimed by some builders, and nobody would dare advertise a draft of more than 12 inches for a rig promoted for the flats.

(A caution here--take all these advertised drafts with a grain of salt. They are often measured with an empty boat, sometimes without fuel or batteries in place. When your rig is loaded with gas, three big batteries and a couple of buddies, it will set several inches lower, and that may be enough to win you a one-night stand with the mosquitoes and no-see-ums if you try to make it run at the advertised depth.)

A poling platform and a pair of powerful, 24-volt trolling motors are standard equipment for chasing fast-moving fish without starting the outboard.

In order to get shallow draft, it's usually necessary to make the aft portions of the bottom fairly flat. In fact, plain old aluminum jon boats will float as high as any $25,000 Kevlar and graphite wonder, in part because of that skillet-flat bottom. (And jon boats make nice tarpon boats, in protected water.)

But flat bottoms are not appealing, either in boats or in women. (Nor in men, my wife hollers from the other room.) In boats, flat bottoms make for a rough ride. I'll drop the analogy here for fear of prosecution.

But in general, the flatter a boat's aft sections, the harder it meets oncoming waves. The deep-vee hull was designed to split the waves and reduce the impact, and it does that beautifully, but it also causes a boat to float very deep in the water. Most deep vees in the 15-20 foot range--the freshwater bass boat is a classic example--will touch bottom in 14 inches of water, and some take a foot-and-a-half to stay afloat--quite a bit for a boat of this size and weight.

The better tarpon boats sit low in the water from bow to stern, so that they don't catch the wind and drift too fast. Most feature a modified vee bottom, often with a transom pocket to feed water to the outboard at full trim.

Also, the deeper the vee, the deeper the motor has to sit in the water in order to get water to the prop and the cooling intake. A motor that sits deep in the water hits bottom in shallow water. Some builders get around this problem, however, by building "pockets" in the aft portions of the hull, just ahead of the transom, to allow water to flow up and back to the lower unit.

Extreme vees are also tippy at rest, which flats fishermen don't like since they frequently walk the gunnels to follow a fish. Vees tend to drop their windward rail in strong winds, which is the opposite of what you want in a low-sided flats rig that probably tends to be wet anyway. And the greater the vee, the more difficult it is to pop most boats up on plane. But flats boats have to get on plane quickly, because the available deep water is often very limited. Thus, lots of vee is a no-no for the ultimate tarpon boat.

Most builders are now producing modified vees with a sharp forward entry and relatively flat aft sections, winding up with that pocket at the transom. This gives a pretty good ride, shallow draft and stability at rest, plus shallow operation at speed. (A little vee also makes a boat track straighter, when it's poled.) Some put a flat "pad" just ahead of the pocket, a miniature planing surface that will add speed to most hulls.

Moving topside, most experts prefer a low freeboard from stem to stern, even though that means it's easier for water to come aboard. Shallow-draft boats with high freeboard "kite"

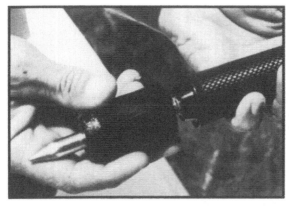

Some guides use replaceable tips on their pushpoles, opting for flat tips on soft mud, non-slipping metal tips over limerock. In either case, the pole must be handled quietly to avoid spooking the fish.

in the wind, drifting rapidly and uncontrollably, and are hard to pole upwind.

Don't take it for granted that any flats boat with low sides will display a minimal freeboard. Some, because of the way they are balanced, have almost no freeboard aft and lots of it forward because they sit on an incline. This is not good, because the boat tends to spin around the axis of the deeper aft section anytime winds blow from the sides. The best designs sit dead flat in the water, displaying the same amount of freeboard pretty much from bow to transom.

The angle of the sides of the boat are also important. Some boats tend to catch the gentle chop of waves in just the wrong way, so that there's a constant slap-slap all day long. It's annoying to anglers, and it definitely puts off fish at times, especially in areas where there's lots of pressure. You can't tell which boats are quiet by looking at them--it takes a test ride.

All flats boat builders will tell you, with a straight face, that their boats will never so much as put a drop of water on your Polaroids in a full gale, but they can't help themselves.

Be advised; in some conditions there just ain't no such thing as a "dry" flats boat.

There are some that do a lot better than others, though. Those with lots of bow flare, extending well aft, tend to keep the spray down better than others. The little 16-foot Dolphin is famous for this, and the Hewes Bonefisher is pretty good, too.

In general, small skiffs need some sort of a spray rail or an extension of the chine forward into the bow area in order to knock down spray that travels up the slopes of the bottom. If bottom meets sides in a smooth flow, the water comes right on up topside and you get very wet.

Any good tarpon boat has loads of storage, because everything has to be secured below decks when a fish is hooked. The boxes should be truly dry in a quality boat, with deep channels to carry off rain and spray before they get below.

You need lots of rod storage, too, horizontal and under the gunnels, so they're not in the way of backcasts. If you're a fly-rodder, remember you need racks that will handle 9-foot rods.

All small skiffs benefit from trim tabs, and these should be standard equipment on tarpon boats because it's often necessary to make long runs over open water to reach the active flats. The tabs allow you to drop the bow to smooth the ride, raise the stern for a quick hole shot, or "cant" the boat to one side or the other to balance a load, or to raise the windward gunnel to make for a dryer ride. They make an enormous difference in tough conditions.

All top-rate flats rigs have hideaway cleats and running lights, so there are no obstructions whatever on the bow deck to snag fly line.

Some of the best-known builders include Action Craft, Dolphin, Hewes, Hoog, Lake & Bay, Maverick, OOSI/Razor, Permit, Renegade and Silver King.

Pushpoles And Poling Platforms

You can get by with a pine dowel as a pushpole, and save a lot of money doing so. But, pine is not durable, nor light, is rarely available in adequate lengths for a tarpon pole, which must often serve to push the boat in depths of 8 feet, and is not easy to sink into the bottom to "stake out" when you want the boat to stay put.

Fiberglass poles offer long life, moderate weight, flexibility and custom foot designs that make life easier. Prices are reasonable, if not inexpensive.

124

Center consoles like this Mako do a good job of chasing tarpon along the beach, in the passes, and in the backwaters. Note that vee-hull boats can best be poled from the bow, as shown here by Keys guide Gil Drake, Jr.

Graphite poles are super-light, strong but flexible, and come with a wide variety of custom feet. Some are even available in sections like Fast Eddie's pool cue--and cost about as much. Graphite poles do shatter on occasion, but many guides feel their lighter weight makes them the pole of choice for all-day use.

Whatever pole you select, get flip-up pole holders to keep it in place. These fold into the gunnels when the pole is in use, preventing snags on the fly line.

Poling platforms generally rise between two and three feet from the aft deck. The farther up you get, the easier it is to see oncoming fish.

Also, the easier it is for them to see you.

Some guys like to be up as high as they can get, some only a couple of feet. Bob Icenogle of Bob's Machine Shop in Ruskin, Fla., solved the problem by attaching his platform to the hydraulic jackplate mechanism on his Evinrude. Bob hits the button and both engine and poling platform go up like an elevator, giving him a choice of a very high position for spotting fish, or a lower position for easier poling and less visibility to fish in clear water.

125

Bay, Beach And Pass Boats For Tarpon

Tarpon are found in many environments other than the flats, of course, and for these more exposed waters larger, deeper boats are more practical.

The classic center-console does a good job in bays and along the beaches, with the smaller versions, up to 20 feet, best for sight-fishing situations. These boats are small enough that they can be moved with the quiet power of an electric trolling motor, yet have plenty of freeboard to allow fishing in substantial seas. Aquasport, Boston Whaler, Grady-White, Hydra-Sports, Mako, ProLine, Stratos and many others make good ones.

For dead-bait fishing, anything right on up to a 53 Hatteras will do, since you wait for the fish to come to you rather than chasing them. In fact, in situations like those encountered off the coast of Texas, you might as well enjoy a big boat all the way, right down to the air conditioning and color TV, since the fish are found well offshore.

And in drift-fishing situations like that in Boca Grande Pass, old-style displacement boats, most of them built of wood planks, are the easiest and most effective to fish. This is because they have lots of keel and lots of weight from their inboard engines, which allows them to drift slowly and keep their low bows into the wind while the skipper fine-tunes with occasional bursts of throttle. Planing hulls, even the big sportfishermen, don't offer the same benefits in that particular fishing situation. Outboards, of course, always drift with their sterns to the wind or current, whichever is stronger, so don't offer the same ease of control in a pass-fishing situation. Many guides also feel that inboards are less disturbing to the fish below than outboards.

Trolling Motors

Tarpon anglers like lots of electrical push, with some guys like Billy Pate clamping up to four 24-volt trolling motors on the transom to get up ramming speed without ever turning on the outboard. More commonly, guides use a pair of 24's on the stern, controlled with switches from the poling platform.

The reason for the seeming excess is that tarpon move rapidly, and seemingly always show up well out of range, and upwind. The only way to reach them consistently without spooking them is with a strong surge of electric propulsion. With some of the better trollers like OMC's largest putting out almost 60 pounds of thrust, you can close the gap in a hurry.

The trolling motor field has shrunk considerably in recent years, and now only three companies produce a full line of electrics. Minn-Kota, Motor Guide and OMC all produce corrosion-proof models that have enough power for tarpon fishing. OMC's are the most powerful, generally the most quiet, and the most durable--but also by far the most expensive.

A unique offering from Navi-Gator shows some promise for tarpon anglers. It's the lower unit, only, of a trolling motor, which clamps right on to the lower unit of your outboard. You steer it by simply turning the steering wheel. When you plane off the boat, the electric rises out of the water, since it's mounted above the cavitation plate. Models with advertised thrust up to 50 pounds are available.

Most anglers use two conventional trollers, one on either side of the poling platform, so that they can steer the boat by alternately running one or the other.

It takes lots of battery power to run these motors, of course. Deep-cycle models are the only way to go, with good ones made by GNB and Delco Voyager. Truly outstanding gel-cel batteries with a life about three times that of conventional acid batteries are available from Sonnenschein and some others, but they are also three times more expensive than the conventional batteries at this writing.

With all this technology aboard, it's not hard to understand how the ultimate tarpon boat can cost well over $20,000--and some are now exceeding $30,000. Fortunately, you can also catch tarpon from a $400 jon boat--or standing on a bridge. Choose your style and have at it.

CHAPTER 17

BIOLOGY AND MANAGEMENT

THE TARPON'S LIFE-DANCE is as complex and as beautiful as that of the salmon, and perhaps even more mysterious. Born into the open sea as tiny, eel-like larvae, the silver darts must find a way to return to their ancestral home along the tropic shores. Most never manage to cross the hundred miles of open ocean. Their time is ephemeral, hours or days, before they too become a part of the fodder of the sea.

But, with each big female releasing up to 19 million of these tiny hopefuls, a few win Nature's lottery. They survive long enough to turn from the bizarre, bodiless "leptocephalus" into silvery minnows, transparent of body, gossamer butterflies drifting in the endless marine universe. Fewer still eventually arrive, almost by chance, at the estuaries.

These forge inland, taking advantage of the inbound tides, hiding in the sea grasses and oyster bars on outgoing, until at last they filter through the mangrove roots to the inch-deep waters where they are safe from the endless chains of snapping jaws.

Many of the most successful bide their time in the shallowest flats at the edge of the estuary, and then on the highest moon tides of summer, leave the sea altogether, swimming over what is normally dry lands to settle into hidden brackish ponds, mosquito ditches and stagnant creeks.

They remain there, safe from the sea predators--though not from the javelin thrust of wading birds and sometimes not from the pollutants of civilization--into their second or third summer. Then, again the spirit moves within them. They take a storm tide and swim back to the sea, leaving behind the safety of the enclosed nursery for the adventure of maturing in the estuary.

Though thousands of anglers from all over the world come to the southeastern United States each year to catch tarpon, relatively little is known about the life-cycle of the silver giants. Much about their migrations, their spawning areas, and their early life-history remain mysterious even to biologists specializing in their study, as well as to anglers who pursue them.

Dr. Roy Crabtree of the Department of Natural Resources Research Labs in St. Petersburg, Florida, is presently concluding a five-year study that he hopes will provide some of the answers on this unique big game species.

Crabtree and graduate student Ned Cyr of the University of South Carolina have provided a few preliminary clues on the results of their findings.

Age And Growth

Judging from Cyr's research, giant fish like those at Homosassa must be among the geriatric set of tarpon. It takes at least 15 years for a tarpon to reach 100 pounds, and the majority of the fish that visit the flats there are larger--and older--than that. In fact, according to both Cyr and Crabtree, growth rate varies wildly on fish in the larger sizes, and can be extremely slow. Some 100-pound fish have been found to be 40 years old.

The much-sought giants of 150 to 200 pounds are probably in their 50's or older. Crabtree notes that virtually all fish over 100 pounds are female. Most male tarpon seem to quit growing at 15 to 20 years of age, at weights between 65 and 90 pounds, even though they may live for many years within that size range.

Females continue to grow heavier, but not proportionately longer, throughout their lives. (How heavy? There's an old report of a tarpon weighing 350 pounds, netted off Hillsboro Inlet in the early part of this century!)

Making sure tarpon survive the catch-and-release process has become an organized affair at the Boca Grande $100,000 Tournament. Fish are fed a mix of pure oxygen and pumped saltwater as scientists and volunteers revive them. The fish are weighed in wet slings which do no damage to internal organs when the tarpon is hoisted out of the water.

But scientists agree that tarpon, unlike snook and grouper, do not appear to change from males to females as they reach extended ages. Apparently the males simply quit growing at around 95 pounds.

Growth in length appears to be fairly rapid in the early years, though it doesn't approach the inch-per-month rates of faster growers like redfish.

A 20.7 inch tarpon caught in the Sebastian River in March of 1989 was held at Mote Marine Labs in Sarasota until October 1 of 1990, by which time it was 27.4 inches long. That particular fish, then, grew about 1/3 inch per month.

In general, Florida tarpon are thought to grow lengthwise rapidly during March through September, but much more slowly from September through February.

The weight of tarpon varies widely within a given length, depending on the sex and condition of the fish, as well as the spawning cycle. A six-foot tarpon can weigh anywhere from 140 to 200 pounds, depending on the girth at the widest area, just ahead of the dorsal fin.

In these days of catch-and-release fishing, the actual weighing of a tarpon is becoming increasingly rare, because lifting the fish completely out of the water often kills it as the internal organs shift. Instead, most anglers estimate the weight, based on a simple formula of length in inches times girth in inches squared, divided by 800:

$$\text{Length} \times \text{Girth}^2 / 800$$

For example, a 72-inch fish with a 40-inch girth will weigh somewhere very close to 144 pounds, while a 72-incher with a 44-inch girth will go about 174 pounds.

The following table has worked out the equation for fish from 60 to 75 inches long, the most common range for tarpon caught by recreational angling:

	GIRTH IN INCHES															
	30	31	32	33	34	35	36	37	38	39	40	41	42	43	44	45
60	68	72	77	82	87	92	97	103	108	114	120					
61	69	73	78	83	88	93	99	104	110	116	122					
62	70	74	79	84	90	95	100	106	112	118	124					
63	71	76	81	86	91	96	102	108	114	120	126					
64	72	77	82	87	92	98	104	110	115	122	128					
65	73	78	83	88	94	100	105	111	117	124	130					
66		79	84	90	95	101	107	113	119	125	132					
67			86	91	97	103	109	115	121	127	134	141				
68				93	98	104	110	116	123	129	136	143				
69					100	106	112	118	125	131	138	145				
70						107	113	120	126	133	140	147	154			
71							115	121	128	135	142	149	157			
72								123	130	137	144	151	159	166		
73									132	139	146	153	161	169	176	
74										141	148	155	163	171	179	187
75											150	158	165	173	181	190

As a general rule, you'll note that the weight goes up about two pounds for every added inch of length, within a given girth size. Adding an inch to girth, on the other hand, can make a much greater difference, 8 to 10 pounds in the largest fish.

132

The girth can quickly be measured by running a loop of light cord around the fish at the thickest section. Mark the spot with a knot, and then take the length similarly with the cord, measuring to the V or fork of the tail, again marking the spot with a knot. Work out the math back at the dock and you'll be within a few pounds of the actual weight, while your tarpon will still be out there swimming.

(It should be noted that for very large fish, the formula tends to underestimate the size. For example, in the spring of 1991 guide Al Dopirak and angler Tom Evans took a pair of new 20-pound-tippet flyrod record fish at Homosassa that considerably bettered the chart. One fish was 74 inches long and had a 43 inch girth, which should have made it weigh about 171. In actuality, it weighed 176.5. The other was 79 inches long and 42 inches in girth, which according to the formula would give a weight of about 174, but that fish actually weighed 180.)

Spawning

Though most guides are convinced that they have seen tarpon spawning in the shallow flats as they "daisy chain" or swim in a circle, biologists thus far have been unable to find any just-spawned tarpon anywhere inside the continental shelf.

Where they do find these fish, only a few hours old, is at the point where the inshore green of the coastal seas ends and the indigo blue of the ocean deeps begin. Along many sections of the Gulf Coast, this is up to 100 miles offshore. Further, the scientists say that the larval tarpon, those just spawned, are not capable of surviving in inshore waters, only in the highly salty offshore waters.

Thus, the scientists conclude that virtually all spawning takes place well offshore. The inshore "chaining" may be a pre-spawn ritual, but they believe that the actual release of eggs only happens when the fish migrate to blue water.

They believe that spawning occurs from April through July in the Gulf, though in Central America tarpon are known to spawn all year. (The last word is not in on this yet--many guides report having seen the actual release of eggs and milt

133

by daisy chaining fish in inshore waters, so biologists may one day learn that spawning occurs inshore as well as off.) Curiously, in places like Boca Grande Pass, thousands of pre-spawn fish show up to feed and sport inshore from May through July, and then show up again--not a hundred miles offshore--but far up the backcountry in water that's more fresh than salt. There's a similar late summer movement into Tampa Bay.

Do the fish from the outside passes and flats make a quick run 100 miles offshore to drop their eggs, then turn around and come back to finish out the summer inside the bays? Given the usual conservation of energy in Nature, this seems doubtful.

Yet, how else can the larval juveniles be explained so far at sea?

These are questions Dr. Crabtree and others will continue to wrestle with in the seasons ahead, just as the guides at Homosassa and elsewhere will wrestle with the daily problem of finding fish for their clients. It's the mystery of the species that intrigues both.

Tarpon produce incredible numbers of eggs, as do most species that spawn in the open sea. According to studies by biologist Ned Cyr, a 65-pound female produces about one million eggs annually, while a 118-pound female studied had an estimated 19.5 million eggs in her ovaries. (The eggs can add up to 15 pounds of weight to a fish of this size.)

Maturity studies are still on-going, but researchers presently estimate that female tarpon require close to 12 years to reach sexual maturity, at which the average fish weighs around 60 pounds. Males mature at a variety of ages beginning no earlier than 7 years, at a minimum size of about 40 pounds.

Baby Tarpon

The minute larvae look more like insects than fish. They are bizarre, big-headed apparitions that have no resemblance whatever to mature tarpon. They are little more than a quarter-inch long when hatched, and appear to grow at about .03 inch per day for around 45 days, at which time they metamorphasize into more fish-like minnows.

134

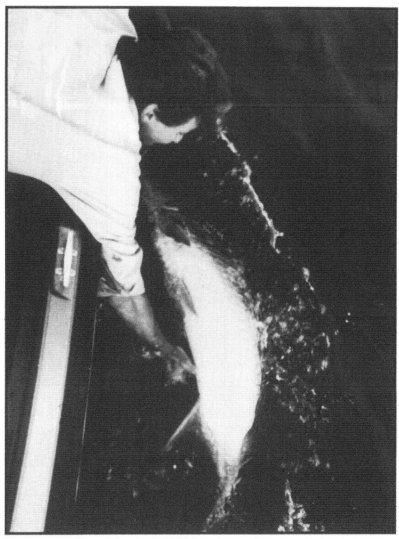

Here as elsewhere, the release ethic has caught on. Tarpon are known to live up to 50 years, so a fish released today may provide angling action for decades of other fishermen.

The few that survive--perhaps only 1 percent of the spawn--ride the tides inshore, where they work their way into brackish estuaries. They appear to seek the extreme backwaters of these regions, stagnant, mangrove-lined ponds that may be filled by high tides only twice monthly on the maximum moon periods. The young fish are not bothered by the low oxygen content, since they can take air directly from the surface. The backwaters make excellent rearing ponds because they're free of most predators found in the deeper sections of the estuaries.

When the fish get big enough to fend for themselves, they evidently ride the high tides back out to more open water, usually at lengths of 14 to 16 inches, and remain in the tidal creeks and mangrove bays until they reach maturity.

Giant Tarpon

The all-tackle record of 283 pounds, taken from Lake Maracaibo, Venezuela, has stood since 1956. No other fish has even come close to displacing this monster, and perhaps none ever will--the second-largest fish in the IGFA records is 248 pounds, 3 ounces, missing the all-tackle mark by more than 30 pounds.

However, some anglers believe that a 300-pound tarpon may exist, and who's to say it doesn't--don't forget that legendary 350-pounder from Hillsboro Inlet.

All of the largest tarpon are females, and females average slightly higher body weight at a given length than males. Nearly all tarpon over 100 pounds have been found to be females, and the tarpon caught by sportfishing methods are more commonly females than males.

Seasonal Migrations

Tarpon are found in water temperatures ranging from the lower 60's to the mid-90's, but their favorite temperature seems to be from 75 to 85. They usually appear on the inshore flats in areas like Homosassa and the Florida Keys in spring when the water first reaches 75, and if there are late cold fronts chilling the water, many move back to deeper water until the temperature rises again.

Similarly, most exit inshore waters in fall, when water temperatures drop with the shorter days and longer nights, and with the coming of the first cold fronts. Tarpon frequently make long coastwise migrations, with fish tagged at Boca Grande showing up both in the Florida Keys and off the Mississippi River Delta in recent years. Tagging studies are still in their infancy, however, so it's too soon to say whether large numbers of fish make these migrations regularly.

The Future

If it takes 50 years to produce a 150-pound tarpon but only an hour to kill such a fish, clearly catch-and-release fishing is the only way to maintain good fishing for large tarpon.

Florida has taken the lead in managing tarpon, predictably since they are the only state with a strong, year around fishery. But there's concern that they have perhaps taken to it a bit late. A tarpon program put into place in 1989 requires purchase of a $50 fee to kill a tarpon. In the first year, the program cut the kill to just 274 from a former estimate of near 5,000, and the following year only 117 were reported killed.

Catch-and-release fishing evidently kills few fish. Dr. Randy Edwards of Mote Marine Laboratories recently studied released fish at Boca Grande via radio-tracking, and of 21 fish tracked, none expired--most returned to the pass within a few hours and resumed normal behavior.

Texas recently passed a law putting an end to all tarpon harvest, though catch-and-release fishing is still legal.

Thus, the drain on the tarpon resource has slowed, but the damage from years past will be with us for a long time to come. The thousands of mature fish killed prior to the permit rule will not be replaced by juvenile fish for decades. Though tarpon fishing remains good throughout much of the southeast, it won't be as good as in the years before widespread harvest until sometime in the next century--and that's assuming that environmental protection agencies keep a tight rein on development of estuarine areas, the essential link in connecting the silver king of the blue water spawn to the green inshore waters where anglers have come to know and love it.

137

Tarpon mounts make breathtaking trophies, but the best mounts by far are not made from the fish themselves, but from carefully painted fiberglass replicas. These replicas last far longer than skin mounts, look better, and do not require the killing of this wonderful gamefish. Enjoy the tarpon, duel with them often, but release each fish to complete its long and remarkable life cycle, and the sport will still be there for your children and theirs to enjoy.

CHAPTER 18

TARPON GUIDES

TARPON GUIDES ARE an unruly lot, mischievous, paranoid, secretive, boisterous and a bit nuts. (OK, you're saying, but how are they any different from outdoors writers?)

They are also maybe the world's finest light tackle anglers, so treat them with respect, despite the fact you suspect them of being just a bit off center. Do not leave your fly box or your wife in the boat with them alone, but listen very carefully to their instructions, even when they are shouted amidst a stream of curses from the poling platform as a 150-pound fish bears down on you.

Tarpon guides are also inclined to mischief, of all sorts, after their day on the water ends. I offer the following anecdote as proof.

Once not so long ago, a half-dozen of the creme de la creme of flats guides, (or maybe the worst of the lot) those with the patience and skill and effrontery to think they can catch the giant spooks off Homosassa in May, were gathered together for the nightly prayer meeting at the Riverside Villas bar. The bar overlooks the river and a tiny dot of land called Monkey Island, so named because for over 20 years it has held a family of semi-tame monkeys.

After several thirst-quenchers, one of the guides studying the monkeys noted that it was a shame the simians were confined on their prison island without ever a thing to drink except the river water. Their only entertainment was walking back and forth, endlessly, on a tight rope suspended between two trees. By general acclaim it was determined that something should be done to correct this injustice.

They rounded up half a dozen oranges from the kitchen and somebody got a hypodermic from his boat, used to inject air into live baits at times, and they proceeded to fill the oranges up with 151-proof rum.

They stood on the docks and threw the oranges over to the island, and the offering was gratefully accepted by the monkeys. Within 30 minutes, the island was a madhouse of screaming, fighting, fornicating apes.

About this time, two unknowing officers of the Florida Marine Patrol docked their boat at the Villas and went ashore for dinner.

The rapscallions in the bar took this in, and no sooner had the officers disappeared around the corner than the guides were back out on the docks. They rigged a piece of rope to the FMP boat, and then poled the other end out to Monkey Island. Lassoed a tree there, and drew the line taut.

The monkeys, used to using such lines for entertainment, quickly investigated.

Two of them made it across to the FMP boat within five minutes, and went at the business of taking out their intoxicated rage by shredding the canvas top and seats, working over the electronics, tossing in the river anything else that would come loose and defecating on anything that would not.

The officers came back to a boat in shambles, and had a very difficult time collaring the disorderly suspects. Meantime, the angelic guides sat at the corner table and looked on, halos over their heads as they wished the patrolmen well.

That incident aside, tarpon guides are special people, maybe the world's finest anglers. They charge substantially for their services, beginning at $300 per day, but they provide decades of know-how and endless hours of backbreaking work for the bucks. A day in their company can turn the rankest amateur into a passable silver king fisherman. The good ones are so much in demand that they often book years in advance, fishing the same anglers in the same weeks season after season. Here's a list of some of the best. (We will not say which, if any, were involved in the monkey caper.)

140

Getting started in tarpon fishing is not easy. A guide can help turn an amateur into an expert in short order. Most provide boat and tackle, plus their expertise and their muscle on the pushpole. Fees range from $300 to $400 daily for flats fishing.

Lee Baker, Marathon, FL, (305) 448-1447
Dave Ballay, Venice, LA, (504) 534-9357
Larry Blue, St. Petersburg, FL (813) 595-4798
Phil Chapman, Lakeland, FL, (813) 646-9445
Charlie Cleveland, Tampa, FL, (813) 935-0241
Mike Collins, Islamorada, FL (305) 852-5837
Babe Darna, Boca Grande, FL (813) 964-2559
Corby Dolar, Homestead, FL, (305) 248-8712
Al Dopirak, Crystal Beach, FL, (813) 785-7774
Ray DeMarco, Anna Maria, FL, (813) 778-9215
Eric Ersch, Satellite Beach, FL, (407) 779-9054
Harlan Franklin, Key West, FL (305) 296-9566
Freddy Futch, Boca Grande, FL (813) 964-2266
Steve Garrett, Miami, FL, (305) 642-6727
Greg Gentile, Port St. Lucie, FL (407)878-0475
Ad Gilbert, Venice, FL (813) 484-8430
Dennis Goldstein, St. Augustine, FL, (904) 825-1971
Paul Hawkins, St. Petersburg, FL, (813) 894-7345
Richard Howard, Clearwater, FL, (813) 446-8962
Van Hubbard, Boca Grande, FL, (813) 697-6944
Jim Hunter, Marathon Shores, FL (305) 289-0941
Cappy Joiner, Boca Grande, FL (813) 697-6052
Lamar Joiner, Boca Grande, FL (813) 697-4939
Joel Kalman, Miami, FL (305) 361-5155
Al Kline, Homosassa, FL (904) 628-5381

Mike Locklear, Homosassa, FL, (904) 628-2602
Dave Markett, Tampa Bay FL, (813) 962-1435
Joe Mauro, Houston, TX, (713) 464-1340
Tim McOsker, St. Petersburg, FL, (813) 797-7715
Larry Mendez, Charolotte Harbor, FL, (813) 874-3474
Bill Miller, Charlotte Harbor, FL, (813) 935-3141
Chris Mitchell, Boca Grande, FL, (813) 964-2887
Scott Moore, Cortez, FL,(813) 778-3005
Phil O'Bannon, Fort Myers, FL, (813) 964-0359
Darrick Parker, Miami, FL, (305) 274-4943
Bub Pritchard, St. Augustine, FL, (904) 824-4347
Glenn Puopolo, Naples, FL, (813) 353-4807
Kenny Shannon, Boca Grande/Venice, FL (813) 497-4876
Bouncer Smith, Pembroke Pines, FL (305) 431-7530
Tom Tamanini, Tampa Bay, FL, (813) 581-4942
Gilbert Vella, Port Isabel, TX, (512) 761-2865
Earl Waters, Homosassa, FL, (904) 628-0333
Mike Williams, Galveston, TX, (713) 723-1911
Phil Woods, Boca Grande, FL, (813) 964-2393
Jon Zorian, Boca Grande, FL, (813) 964-2038

As a final note, there are two very good guides associations in Florida which specialize in tarpon fishing. One is the Boca Grande Guides Association, at Boca Grande Pass, which publishes an excellent how-to brochure on fishing the pass, with a complete list of guides' phone numbers. Send a self-addressed, stamped envelope to P.O. Box 676, Boca Grande, FL 33921.

The other is the Florida Keys Guides Association, which includes most of the inshore guides throughout the Keys. Contact is Mike Collins at (305) 852-5837.

To explore the excellent fishing throughout Central America, contact Pan Angling at (800) 533-4353; Trek Safaris at (800) 654-9915 or Fishing Adventures at (800)336-9735.

For video instruction in tarpon fishing, you might consider Capt. Bill Miller's excellent "Complete Guide To Tarpon Fishing With Artificials." The 50-minute tape provides in-depth instruction, plus lots of live action. It's $29.95 from MB Outdoor Ventures, Dept. LOP, P.O. Box 261358, Tampa, FL 33685.

CHAPTER 19

FEAR'S LURE

(Editor's Note: There's more to tarpon fishing than tarpon, or fishing. The following story we offer as a finale that perhaps catches some of the mystique of pursuing these grand fish. An earlier version of the story had the distinction of having been printed--and reprinted-- several times in Florida Sportsman Magazine since it was written in 1975. The story is fictional, but based on a true incident that occurred in the Keys in the early 70's.)

The fisherman stood in the small white boat and saw the gigantic tarpon, and wondered. An incredible fish, casting a shadow like a dirigible on the white sand bottom. A hulking monster that would certainly weigh--what? Two-fifty? Maybe more. It looked more than a foot wide between the eyes.

Three hundred. Could it be?

It hung still in against the edge of white flat, ponderous, immobile, green barnacles--yes, barnacles--growing on its back like a whale. The tide was nearly gone. Scarcely enough water for the fish to swim in.

Perhaps the tarpon was old and looking for a safe place to finish its days away from the great brown sharks out in the emerald channel. Perhaps this giant of all tarpon was independent of the ways of its species. Maybe that was why it had grown so big. Maybe it always fed on the shallow edge of the reef at low tide, even though this was not the way of other tarpon.

Or perhaps, he would think later, it had been somehow ordained that the fish would be there, and that he would meet it, for reasons he would never finally understand.

It was there. That was all that mattered, a fish heavy as a bear and as long as a porpoise and made of steel. He thought that he had never seen anything quite so clearly in his life, as that nearly transparent fish in the transparent water.

It did not see him, or if it did, chose to ignore him as he prepared to cast. He would hook the fish on a 300-yard strand on monofilament that would lift only 15 pounds straight up.

The wooden plug bobbed lightly as it splashed down, and he could see the heavy trebles that bristled from its stomach in the clear water. He thought that he should have been nervous as he brought the lure over the fish, but he was not. He was sure that it would take, and that he would beat it, though he could not know what would happen after.

Sure enough. The tarpon rolled up lazily and took the lure down with a slow, elephantine sweep of its head, and the boil was no larger than that made by a small and hurried barracuda. He set the hook, and it lodged in the tarpon's bony jaw.

It was off, leaving only a white swirl of marl where it had accelerated, and the line was running free and smooth from the reel, slicing the water with the sound of silk ripping. The fish did not jump then, as is the way of smaller fish, nor did it ever except at the end. Soon it was very far away and again he was alone in the small white boat.

Without the steady cry of the reel he could almost have believed the fish was imaginary, that it had never been there at all. The sea was peaceful, and frigate birds wheeled like sleepy vultures in the shimmering heat of the July sky.

He did not touch the drag as the tarpon streaked out across the shoals, and steadily, the increasing pressure began to work on the light boat. The fish was going with the tide, and slowly the boat began to follow, finally gaining momentum until the drag almost stopped slipping altogether.

They moved east toward Looe Key, where the land fell away to the inky blue of the open sea beyond. He held the rod low, the butt jammed against his belt buckle and his arms out straight, and tried not to notice the growing ache in his forearms and shoulders.

144

"Getting old," he had to admit. "Getting too old."

Once, when the bare spool began to show, he started the motor and ran after the fish until he had back his margin of safety, then shut down again and let the fish pull.

When it reached the lime-green shoals at the inside of the reef the line slackened, and he could see the fish coming toward the boat very fast. Suddenly it was towering up above him, head down, body arched, the baseball-big eye staring at him from ten feet away, hanging in the air as though time had stopped.

It would hang there forever, burned into his brain, long after the other, the part that was still to come, had begun to fade.

Then it was gone, back in the water and down, far beyond the outside edge of the brown reef, out where the earth fell away forever and the water turned indigo. It swam straight down for 200 feet, then stopped. The man strained the line until it began to hum, but the fish did not move. Sweat ran down his forehead and streaked his Polaroids, and he began to envy the fish so far below in the cool, blue depths.

He held steady pressure, and finally the tarpon gave, and he began to pump. After a long time it came to the top and shoved its bucket-sized head through the surface, but then dived again.

Working slowly, grunting, aching, he pumped the fish up once more. It held, about 30 feet off, until he finally pulled it over on its back, and then it let go a stream of bubbles, as though its lungs had burst, and then it seemed to be over.

The fish lay on its side, much bigger than the man and almost as big as the skiff, and 25 times heavier than the line that had beaten it.

He carried only a small lip gaff. He had kept only one other tarpon, freeing all the rest, and had never needed a big killing hook until now. The bite was scarcely broad enough to fit around the fish's lip, but it did.

He set the point and began to lift. He had the head and shoulders over the gunnel when the fish lunged.

The gaff jerked out of its wooden handle, and the fish plunged back into the water. When it did, two of the big stainless steel barbs on the plug lanced into the palm of his hand like silver fangs.

He did not cry out when the hooks went home, but grunted short and low like a man who has been hit in the stomach when he is not expecting it. The fish lay awash and still, as solidly hooked to the rear of the plug as the man was to the front. The tarpon's weight bent him over the gunnel. Blood dripped off his thumb and into the water to join the delicate pink stain from the fish.

When he reached down to work the hooks out with his free hand he found that he could not get to them and still keep himself inside the boat.

He tried to pull the tarpon closer, straining against the bite of the hooks, but before he could get its head out of the water, he could feel one of the points scraping across bone inside his hand, and then the sun pressed down on him, and then things went dark.

He dreamed of a cool evening when they were young and could not die. They had gone down to Spanish Harbor to watch the tide run out. They went down the white limestone path in the moonlight, and crabs large as rabbits scuttled into the brush ahead of them. They had gone down to look at the sea often then, when he was still in awe of it.

A gas lantern hung from a nail driven into the slimy beam of the sea wall and illuminated the milky green tide as it ran down the hill to the Atlantic.

"Shrinks you can see troo," said the old Cuban who sat behind the lantern. He held up one of the transparent-brown crustaceans to the white fire of the mantle. In the darkness under the bridge, a school of 80-pounders were wallowing like silver hogs as they ambushed the shrimp coming down the channel.

"The black spot," he touched the head where the spine began, "is the heart." He smiled at her as he pinched off the head. He dropped the tail into a tin pail full of ice, then took a long, thoughtful drink from the wine bottle between his legs. The tail rattled against the pail, then was still.

"How can you?" his wife had asked.

"Señora?"

146

"Kill them like that?"

The Cuban considered it. A serious question. He spoke seriously.

"All things come to an end. You, even. The babies you will make, even." He took another drink. "Even I. It is the black that allows us to understand white, the frigate bird that makes us love the albatross. I only complete their lives."

Almost as he finished speaking a pair of shrimp floated by, and like moths to flame zagged their way toward the lantern. The old man obligingly netted and beheaded them and drank again.

"You see?" he grinned. Red eyes, like a demon, in the lantern glow. A tarpon rolled mightily under the bridge. "And, I save them from worse, from the fish."

"You call this saving?"

"I save them . . . from fear," the old man said at last.

"Your net is the end for them, all the same."

And the old man, speaking slowly and quietly in the cool dream of moonlight, said, "So. But, the fear is the bad thing, not the dying. The shrink, he is afraid of the sabalo. Each night when the sun goes down and the tide start to pull, he is scared, very bad. If he make it tonight, tomorrow night the same, and again, until they get him. But he is not afraid of the light. He sees the light and he thinks: the sun-now I am safe again. They come to me, and I net them, and it is a good way and a fearless way for them to finish." He emptied the bottle.

All of the time he had been speaking he was watching the water, and suddenly like a heron striking he shot the net down to scoop up another shrimp.

"No fear," he grinned as he dropped the flipping tail into the bucket.

They had made babies. One had died, the other grown and moved to California, and did not write. His wife had died, too. So. The old Cuban had it right.

The heat came again and he was awake. He had rolled onto his back, with the hooked arm stretched over his head and his shoulders arched across the gunnel. His eyes opened to the fierce brilliance of the afternoon sky. A black frigate bird wheeled slowly in the windless depths overhead.

147

The fish was still, and he thought is must have died. It lay on its side, not seeming to move at all. The blood on his hand had clotted to thin, black ribbons. Where the water washed at it clouds of silver minnows swarmed.

There was water in the cooler at the other end of the boat, but he could not reach it. Few places are drier than the sea when you want fresh water, and he was beginning to want it badly. The metal cooler would be too hot to touch on the outside, but inside the jug was resting against a clear block of ice that would have melted by now to cradle the shape of the sweating glass.

He reached out dangerously far and got his hand on the plug, but could not risk the extra two inches it would have taken to get a grip on the hooks. He pulled on the lure to draw the fish closer. When he did, the tarpon responded with a slow motion of its tail, and its gills began to pump.

It was alive, beginning to regain its strength steadily and surely.

The man shook and pushed and pulled at the plug, but the hooks held fast. The fish slowly righted itself and began to fin along with the northeasterly flow of the stream. Before long it would be strong enough to pull him out of the boat, he knew.

He tore at the plug and swore, but the hooks clung to his palm as if they had grown there.

The tarpon was swimming steadily with the drift of the boat, its power coming back rapidly. He expected it to explode in a violent effort, and he braced himself each time it moved in any way different from the effortless glide that kept it flowing with the current.

There was no drama when it came. It seemed to happen in slow motion. The fish simply swept its head to one side, and the man could not hold back any more than if he had been hitched to a draft horse. He made a desperate lunge for the gunnel when he first hit the water, spouting saltwater, trying to see, but he could not reach it.

The tarpon moved away from the boat, still at the surface and swimming slowly, not alarmed by him in the water beside it. The rod was in the gimbal with the drag backed off for the gaffing, and now the fish took line easily against its light tension.

He found that he could reach the hooks at last. He worked them frantically with his free hand, first trying to back them out, then to rip them through the flesh. But they were set in the tough muscle of the palm and would not budge.

They had gone better than a hundred yards when the fish started down. He caught a good breath, but did not expect to come up again as he saw the water darken over him. Silver bubbles rushed by and the shovel-sized tail buffeted him as they slid down toward the cold, cobalt darkness below. He threw a leg over the fish's back and grabbed the upper jaw with his free hand, pulling madly. The tarpon kept on diving.

He became sure then that he would not make it, and with the certainty felt the dread go out of him like air from a balloon. The seconds seemed to open into hours as the growing pressure drummed at his ears. The fear is the bad thing, he heard the old Cuban say. All things must come to an end. It seemed somehow right that he should be here with the fish.

He relaxed and looked around, into the blue space, the indigo universe of the open sea. He looked at the tiny sea lice flowing on the tarpon's back, and the barnacles that crusted like mossy warts on its back, at the great chain-mail flow of its silver side in the blue and enormous light.

He wondered if men or sharks would find him first, and what his wife would do, and what the sea water would feel like in his lungs. None of it seemed to matter very much, at all. He decided to try the plug a final time, and then to let go of his air.

He pulled with all his strength, but it was no good. Strong hooks, well made. They held what they hooked.

He rode his silver steed through the gathering dusk of the deep.

Pulled again. Why?

Why not?

And the fish responded. It shook itself like a wet dog, quivering all over. He pulled again. Something slipped.

The plug was giving up its air. Little bubbles, being forced out of the wood by the pressure. Little silver bubbles, going up toward the surface where he could not go.

He pulled again, a little, no longer caring.

And suddenly the hook gave, and the plug snapped out of the tarpon's mouth.

He sat on its back a long moment, looking at the plug in his hand, not wanting to do anything but sit there, continue the ride to the blue horizon.

Then he was going up toward the light and the sun, dizzied, going up a long time toward the incredible brightness. Coming out in an brilliant explosion of silver water. Letting his air go too soon and taking a mouthful of water with the first gulps of air at the surface. Sweet, sweet salt air.

After he stopped coughing, he looked for the boat. It hung far away at the very end of the line, bobbing like a cork in the growing chop.

The plug still clung to his hand. He pulled gently on the shock leader, and then on the line, and slowly the boat began to come to him or he to it, it was hard to tell which was moving. He worked his way up the line. Hung on the boat a long time, and finally pulled himself over the transom.

He lay on his back and stared into the depths of the sky. The frigate bird still circled, now a vague black dot far away over the blue hills of the Stream, but not quite out of sight. It would never again be quite out of sight, he knew.

But somehow, it did not seem so important any more.

FISHING & HUNTING
RESOURCE DIRECTORY

If you are interested in more productive fishing and hunting trips, then this info is for you!

Larsen's Outdoor Publishing is the publisher of several quality Outdoor Libraries - all informational-type books that focus on how and where to catch America's most popular sport fish, hunt America's most popular big game or travel to productive or exciting destinations.

The perfect-bound, soft-cover books include numerous illustrative

graphics, line drawings, maps and photographs. The BASS SERIES LIBRARY and the two HUNTING LIBRARIES are nationwide in scope. The INSHORE SERIES covers coastal areas from Texas to Maryland and foreign waters. The OUTDOOR TRAVEL SERIES covers the most popular fishing and diving destinations in the world. The BASS WATERS SERIES focuses on the top lakes and rivers in the nation's most visited largemouth bass fishing state.

All series appeal to outdoorsmen/readers of all skill levels. The unique four-color cover design, interior layout, quality, information content and economical price makes these books hot sellers in the marketplace. Best of all, you can learn to be more successful in your outdoor endeavors!!

THE BASS SERIES LIBRARY
by Larry Larsen

1. FOLLOW THE FORAGE FOR BETTER BASS ANGLING
VOL. 1 BASS/PREY RELATIONSHIP
Learn how to determine the dominant forage in a body of water, and you will consistently catch more and larger bass. Whether you fish artificial lures or live bait, your bass stringer will benefit!

2. FOLLOW THE FORAGE FOR BETTER BASS ANGLING
VOL. 2 TECHNIQUES
Learn why one lure or bait is more successful than others and how to use each lure under varying conditions. You will also learn highly productive patterns that will catch bass under most circumstances!

3. BASS PRO STRATEGIES
Professional fishermen know how changes in pH, water temperature, color and fluctuations affect bass fishing, and they know how to adapt to weather and topographical variations. Learn from their experience. Your productivity will improve after spending a few hours with this compilation of tactics!

4. BASS LURES - TRICKS & TECHNIQUES
When bass become accustomed to the same artificials and presentations seen over and over again, they become harder to catch. Learn how to rig or modify your lures and develop specific presentation and retrieve methods to spark or renew the interest of largemouth!

5. SHALLOW WATER BASS
Bass spend 90% of their time in the shallows, and you spend the majority of the time fishing for them in waters less than 15 feet deep. Learn specific productive tactics that you can apply to fishing in marshes, estuaries, reservoirs, lakes, creeks and small ponds. You'll likely triple your results!

THE BASS SERIES LIBRARY
by Larry Larsen

6. BASS FISHING FACTS

Learn why and how bass behave during pre- and post-spawn, how they utilize their senses and how they respond to their environment, and you'll increase your bass angling success! This angler's guide to the lifestyles and behavior of the black bass is a reference source never before compiled. It examines how bass utilize their senses to feed. By applying this knowledge, your productivity will increase for largemouth as well as Redeye, Suwannee, Spotted and other bass species.

7. TROPHY BASS

If you're more interested in wrestling with one or two monster largemouth than with a "panfull" of yearlings, then learn what techniques and habitats will improve your chances. This book takes a look at geographical areas and waters that offer better opportunities to catch giant bass, as well as proven methods and tactics for both man made and natural waters. The "how to" information was gleaned from professional guides and other experienced trophy bass hunters.

8. ANGLER'S GUIDE TO BASS PATTERNS

Catch bass every time out by learning how to develop a productive pattern quickly and effectively. Learn the most effective combination of lures, methods and places. Understanding bass movement and activity and the most appropriate and effective techniques to employ will add many pounds of enjoyment to the sport of bass fishing.

9. BASS GUIDE TIPS

Learn the most productive methods of top bass fishing guides in the country and secret techniques known only in a certain region or state that may work in your waters. Special features include shiners, sunfish kites & flies; flippin, pitchin' & dead stickin' rattlin; skippin' & jerk baits; moving, deep, hot & cold waters; fronts, high winds & rain. New approaches for bass angling success!

INSHORE SERIES
byFrankSargeant

IL1. THE SNOOK BOOK
"Must" reading for anyone who loves the pursuit of this unique sub-tropic species. Every aspect of how you can find and catch big snook is covered, in all seasons and all waters where snook are found.

IL2. THE REDFISH BOOK
Packed with expertise from the nation's leading redfish anglers and guides, this book covers every aspect of finding and fooling giant reds. You'll learn secret techniques revealed for the first time.

IL3. THE TARPON BOOK
Find and catch the wily "silver king" along the Gulf Coast, north through the mid-Atlantic, and south along Central and South American coastlines. Numerous experts share their most productive techniques.

IL4. THE TROUT BOOK - *COMING SOON!*
You'll learn the best seasons, techniques and lures in this comprehensive book.

OUTDOOR TRAVEL SERIES
by Timothy O'Keefe and Larry Larsen

A candid guide with inside information on the best charters, time of the year, and other vital recommendations that can make your next fishing and/or diving trip much more enjoyable.

OT1. FISH & DIVE THE CARIBBEAN - Volume 1
Northern Caribbean, including Cozumel, Caymans Bahamas, Virgin Islands and other popular destinations.

OT2. FISH & DIVE THE CARIBBEAN - Volume 2 - *COMING SOON!* Southern Caribbean, including Guadeloupe, Bonaire, Costa Rica, Venezuela and other destinations.

DEER HUNTING LIBRARY

by John E. Phillips

DH1. MASTERS' SECRETS OF DEER HUNTING
Increase your deer hunting success significantly by learning from the masters of the sport. New information on tactics and strategies for bagging deer is included in this book, the most comprehensive of its kind.

DH2. THE SCIENCE OF DEER HUNTING - *COMING SOON!*

TURKEY HUNTING LIBRARY

by John E. Phillips

TH1. MASTERS' SECRETS OF TURKEY HUNTING
Masters of the sport have solved some of the most difficult problems you will encounter while hunting wily longbeards with bows, blackpowder guns and shotguns. Learn 10 deadly sins of turkey hunting and what to do if you commit them.

TH2. OUTSMART TOUGH TURKEYS - *COMING SOON!*

BASS WATERS SERIES

by Larry Larsen

Take the guessing game out of your next bass fishing trip. The most productive bass waters in each region of the state are described in this multi-volume series, including boat ramp information, seasonal tactics, water characteristics and much more. Popular and overlooked lakes, rivers, streams, ponds, canals, marshes and estuaries are clearly detailed with numerous maps and drawings.

BW1. GUIDE TO NORTH FLORIDA BASS WATERS
From Orange Lake north and west.

BW2. GUIDE TO CENTRAL FLORIDA BASS WATERS
From Tampa/Orlando to Palatka.

BW3. GUIDE TO SOUTH FLORIDA BASS WATERS
COMING SOON! - from I-4 to the Everglades.